# NO SUPPLIES ReQuired

## Crowdbreakers & Games

by Dan McGill

**Group**

Loveland, Colorado

## Acknowledgments

How can I begin to thank all the great minds behind the group games tradition? A dozen names come to mind, and I know there are hundreds more: publishers, writers, youth ministers, camp directors, lovers of fun. Then there are all the kids who come to me with great new game ideas and the geniuses who figure out how to play old games in new ways. Thanks to every one! Finally, thanks to the people who've worked with me: the volunteers, staff members, and especially the kids. And I could never have done this without my wife, Lawana, and my children, Megan and Brendan.—D. M.

# NO SUPPLIES REQUIRED CROWDBREAKERS AND GAMES

Copyright ©1995 Dan McGill

### Credits
Book Acquisitions Editor: Mike Nappa
Editors: Stephen Parolini and Candace McMahan
Senior Editor: Dan Benson
Creative Products Director: Joani Schultz
Copy Editor: Bob Buller
Art Director/Designer: Jean Bruns
Cover Art Director: Janet Barker
Computer Graphic Artist: Bill Fisher
Cover Photographer: Bill Denison
Illustrator: RoseAnne Buerge
Production Manager: Gingar Kunkel

### Library of Congress Cataloging-in-Publication Data
McGill, Daniel J., 1955-
  No-supplies-required crowdbreakers and games / by Dan McGill.
    p.  cm.
  ISBN 1-55945-700-7
  1. Group games. 2. Amusements. 3. Youth—Recreation.  I. Title.
  GV1201.M424  1995
790.1'92—dc20                                                                95-16195
                                                                             CIP

10  9  8  7             04  03  02  01  00
Printed in the United States of America.

Visit our Web site: www.grouppublishing.com

# NO SUPPLIES · REQUIRED CONTENTS

# BEFORE YOU PLAY...

# CROWDBREAKERS AND GAMES

## I. Introductions . . . . . . . . . . . . . . . . . . . . . . . . . . . . . . . .14

NO SUPPLIES · REQUIRED ·

BEFORE YOU BEFORE PLAY...

## WHAT MAKES THIS GAME BOOK DIFFERENT?

I love simplicity. I love games that are fun and *easy* to play. Throughout my 15 years in youth ministry, I've looked for a book of games I could take anywhere, without worrying about the supplies I would need to play them. Now my dream has finally come true with this game book.

Can you have fun without supplies? This book answers a resounding yes to that question.

I've used supply-free games (and supply-intensive games) for years, and when I look back on my career I am surprised to find that the most memorable games I ever played required nothing but people.

While writing this book, I discovered another, perhaps more compelling, reason for a book of supply-free games: You can take it anywhere. I can't count the number of times I've been on a retreat or a trip and wished that I had my office full of books and supplies with me. In that sense, *No-Supplies-Required Crowd-breakers and Games* is a form of travel insurance.

Take this book, gather up your group members, and go have some fun. Forget the volleyball net, flying discs, and softball equipment—you don't need any supplies. This book will save *you* time, your *budget* money, and the *earth* wasted resources.

And you'll have fun in the process. What could be better?

## A WORD TO THE GAME MASTER (THAT'S YOU, THE LEADER!)

The key ingredient for making these or any other games work is to remember that you, the Game Master, are in charge. You can stop the game, change the time, alter the rules, or do whatever is necessary to have a fun and safe time.

As Game Master, you must be ready to shift gears quickly. And you'll need to learn how to read your group's interest level. Sometimes kids groan at the prospect of a new game but end up cheering for more before it's over. Other times they cheer the game's concept but grow bored or lose interest before the final whistle. When kids show interest in a game, extend your playing time. But if a game drags on, shorten it before kids threaten mutiny. Improvise new rules and strategies whenever necessary and be prepared to adapt to different kinds of weather. And don't forget that your kids often have great ideas, too. Use their ideas to make your games even more fun!

Finally, vary the types of games you use with your group. Try some crazy games. Try some serious or thought-provoking games. The more emotions your kids experience, the closer your group will grow together.

## CHOOSING PLAYERS AND FORMING TEAMS

There are many ways to choose players and form teams. (Check out the games in "Game Chest" on pages 41-43 as one example.) Don't get stuck in the same old rut. Make choosing teams fun! Here are a few suggestions:

### Choosing Single Players
- Pick the loudest person in the crowd.
- Count the number of group members and secretly pick a number between one and the number in the group. Then have each group member choose a different number between one and the number in the group. The person who chooses the number you picked is "It."
- Pick any date in the year and choose the person whose birthday comes closest to that date.
- Pick the first person to laugh, speak, or move (after you give a signal).

### Forming Pairs
- Have kids choose their own partners.
- Form pairs of kids with similar colors of clothing.
- Pair up kids whose birthdays are closest to each other.
- Have kids tell their favorite colors, flavors of ice cream,

school subjects, musical styles, or movies. Then pair up kids who have the same (or similar) favorites. Or pair up kids who have different favorites.

● Pair up kids whose names are next to each other in alphabetical order.

### Creating Small Groups

Have kids mill around the room and form groups based on one of the following criteria. Find everyone in this room who

● was born in the same month or in the same season,

● has the same length of hair,

● has the same color of eyes,

● has the same color of socks, or

● has the same type of shoes.

If one group is much larger than others, choose a different criterion and start again or simply move a few members of the large group to other groups.

**FUN, NO-SUPPLIES PRIZES** What are games without prizes? Actually, games are often just as fun without prizes as with them. But sometimes a prize can help motivate kids and get them excited about a game. Since this is a book of no-supplies games, here are a few no-supplies prizes to build kids' excitement for game time.

### Individual Prizes

● Give the winner a ride around the playing area on everyone else's shoulders.

● Let the winner be first in line at the next meal.

● Excuse the winner from an unwanted task such as doing dishes on a retreat.

● Give the winner a round of applause or three cheers.

● Award the winner a title of honor. Be creative!

● Give the winner a more responsible position in the next game.

● Let the winner choose the next activity.

● Award the winner a handshake from everyone in the group.

● Have the rest of the group sing the winner's favorite song.

● Let the winner choose the toppings for your next pizza party.

● Award the winner a coveted seat in a vehicle on your next trip.

● Designate a comfortable chair the "winner's chair" and let only the winner sit in it.

● Have everyone give the winner a quick back rub (if he or she wants one).

● Let the winner softly pat everyone else on the head.

● Have everyone gently give the winner a pat on the back.

● Sing "Happy Birthday" to the winner.

### Small-Group or Team Prizes

● Have the entire class pause for a few seconds of silence every time the leader calls the winning team's name during the rest of the meeting.

● Let the winning team leave five minutes early or stay five minutes late to plan the entire group's next fun activity.

● Have members of the winning team stand and give themselves a cheer at the next meeting.

● Let the members of the winning team choose the seats they want on the bus or van during your next trip.

● Let the winning team pick the restaurant for your group to visit (within budget limits).

● Adapt any of the individual prizes above for a team. For example, the entire team can line up first for the next meal at a retreat.

### Group Prizes

When the entire group accomplishes a task together or competes with good sportsmanship,

● award the group extra sleep on a retreat, more free time during a meeting, or a chance to repeat a favorite game or activity;

● have group members give each other a cheer;

● have group members participate in a group hug; or

● have group members choose a song for the leaders to sing in honor of their victory or accomplishment.

# CROWDBREAKERS & GAMES

NO SUPPLIES · REQUIRED ·

# A Little About Yourself

**NUMBER OF PLAYERS:** Any number

**LOCATION:** Any space large enough for everyone in the group to stand or sit in a circle

**THE GAME:** Choose one of the following questions or statements, then have kids introduce themselves by stating their names and responses to the question or statement.

- What is the loudest noise you've ever heard?
- What is your earliest memory?
- What is one thing you hope will happen in this group?
- Name all of the places you have lived.
- What is the funniest movie scene you've seen?
- Tell about a nickname you had as a child.
- Describe the most extreme weather condition you've been in.
- Name one good thing that has happened in another group you have been in.
- Where is your favorite place in nature?
- What is your middle name, or what do you think it should have been?
- Describe the best meal you've ever eaten.
- What's your favorite song? (To add some risk, ask kids to sing a few bars.)
- Describe the most unusual thing that's happened to you.
- What's the best thing a friend ever told you?
- What's the worst chore you've ever had?

Select a new question or statement each time you meet with kids.

# CTIONS

*In this chapter you'll find activities to jump-start your meeting, introduce strangers, and reacquaint friends. Use these nonthreatening games and crowdbreakers to help your kids learn more about each other.*

## ACROSTIC

**NUMBER OF PLAYERS:** Any number

**LOCATION:** Any space large enough for everyone in the group to stand or sit in a circle

**THE GAME:** An acrostic is an arrangement of words in which certain letters in each line, when taken in order, spell out a word or motto. Ask group members to introduce themselves to each other by using words or phrases that describe them to create acrostics of their own names (or nicknames). For example:

| | | |
|---|---|---|
| Dynamic | or | Tried and true |
| Independent | | Oh boy, a boy! |
| Able | | Diamond in the rough |
| No-nonsense | | Destined for glory |
| Enthusiastic | | |

**VARIATION:** Have kids mix up the order of the letters in their names. Then have the rest of the group attempt to figure out each name.

## ALTER EGO

**NUMBER OF PLAYERS:** Any number

**LOCATION:** Any space large enough for everyone in the group to stand or sit in a circle

**THE GAME:** Ask kids to introduce themselves and tell the group who they would most like to be other than themselves. They may name fictional characters or actual people, either living or dead. For example, kids could name Jean-Luc Picard from *Star Trek: The Next Generation,* Meryl Streep, Michael Jordan, or Joan of Arc. Kids should not explain their choices. Allow kids to enjoy the mystery of the "why" behind each other's choices.

**VARIATION:** Have kids introduce themselves as the characters or persons they'd like to be and tell their real names later in the meeting or event.

# ANIMAL KINGDOM

**NUMBER OF PLAYERS:** Six or more

**LOCATION:** Any space large enough for everyone in the group to start the game by standing or sitting in a circle

**THE GAME:** Ask kids to introduce themselves and say which of the following animals they most identify with: eagle, dolphin, lion, sparrow, whale, or unicorn. (Use fewer animals for groups of 10 or fewer.)

Then have kids group themselves according to the animals they chose. (Combine the two smallest groups if either has fewer than three members.) Direct kids to answer the following three questions in their small groups.

● **What is one thing all of you have experienced that many other people have not?**
● **What is one thing all of you believe in?**
● **What is one thing all of you are afraid of?**

Then ask teenagers to discover something each group member has done that no one else in the group has done. Have volunteers summarize their groups' answers to the questions and share the unique experiences of their group members.

# COMEDY HOUR

**NUMBER OF PLAYERS:** Any number

**LOCATION:** Anywhere

**THE GAME:** Form pairs. Ask each partner to complete any three of the following sentences:

- **The funniest television commercial I've seen this year is** . . .
- **The most needlessly repeated phrase a parent or teacher ever used with me is** . . .
- **The best** (clean) **joke I've heard recently is** . . .
- **The funniest person I've ever met is** . . .
- **The funniest face I've ever seen someone make is** . . . (Have kids attempt to create them for their partners.)
- **The best practical joke I've heard of is** . . .

# DREAM VACATION

**NUMBER OF PLAYERS:** Any number

**LOCATION:** Anywhere

**THE GAME:** Form pairs of people who don't know each other well. Then read the following scenario and have kids discuss their responses to it. Say:

**You've just won a dream vacation for two. You can travel to any destination in the world and stay there for two weeks, and all your expenses will be covered. However, there is one requirement: You must choose a destination that will help fulfill your life's goals. That is, it must be a place that reflects the purpose or direction of your life as you hope to live it in the future.**

Allow pairs time to discuss their vacation choices and why they'd choose them. Then have kids announce their choices to the entire group. Allow time for teenagers to ask each other why they chose their locations.

# FAMILY TREE

**NUMBER OF PLAYERS:** Any number

**LOCATION:** Anywhere

**THE GAME:** Form pairs of group members not related to each other. Then have each pair create a fictional family tree that shows how the partners really are long-lost relatives descended from a famous ancestor (real or fictional). Have kids tell the entire group about their famous ancestors.

During the rest of the meeting, have kids refer to each other by their famous ancestors' names. For example, if a pair claims to have descended from Cleopatra, call them "the children of Cleopatra."

# FIVE AROUND THE CIRCLE

**NUMBER OF PLAYERS:** Eight or more

**LOCATION:** Any space large enough for everyone in the group to sit in a circle

**THE GAME:** Have everyone sit in a circle. Ask a volunteer to introduce himself or herself and the four people on his or her left to the rest of the group.

Then the volunteer may ask one of the four people he or she introduced to switch places with anyone else in the circle (except for the five just introduced). The person who takes the previously introduced person's place must then introduce himself or herself and the four people to his or her left. Continue until everyone is able to introduce everyone else.

For smaller groups, have kids introduce just one or two persons.

# I KNOW ALL ABOUT YOU

**NUMBER OF PLAYERS:** Any number

**LOCATION:** Anywhere

**THE GAME:** Form pairs of people who don't know each other well. Have partners take turns guessing each other's most exciting and memorable experiences. Allow plenty of freedom for creativity, but tell kids that they are to suggest only positive descriptions of their partners' experiences.

Then have partners explain to each other which guesses were and were not accurate. Allow a few minutes for partners to describe some of the true events in their lives that were not guessed.

After partners have guessed and responded, have them take turns introducing each other to the entire group.

# INTERROGATE THE LEADERS

**NUMBER OF PLAYERS:** 10 or more

**LOCATION:** Anywhere

**THE GAME:** Form the same number of groups as you have leaders or adult sponsors. Assign a leader to each group and have group members "grill" the leader with as many questions as they can in five minutes or less. Then have volunteers from the small groups introduce their leaders or sponsors to the entire group.

# LEFT OUT AND LONELY

**NUMBER OF PLAYERS:** Any number

**LOCATION:** Anywhere

**THE GAME:** This activity works best in groups in which participants are comfortable sharing intimate thoughts.

Form pairs, trios, or small groups and ask each group member to respond to the following statements:

● **Describe a time you were left out of some fun or excitement because you were too young.**

- Describe a time you finally got to do something because you were old enough.
- Describe a time you felt lonely because you didn't have a friend or because you had just lost one.
- Describe a time you finally made a friend after being lonely.

# NAME ROVER

**NUMBER OF PLAYERS:** 12 to 24 (Form several groups if you have more than 24 players.)

**LOCATION:** Any room large enough for two rows of kids to line up across from each other

**THE GAME:** Have kids quickly say their names to the group (the faster the better). Then form two teams—team 1 and team 2— and have them face each other from opposite sides of the room.

Have the person on the right end of team 1's line call out the name of the person on the right end of team 2's line. If he or she correctly identifies this person, that person must go to the left end of team 1's line. But if he or she incorrectly identifies the person, the person from team 2 must say his or her real name and move to the left end of his or her own line.

Then have the person on the right end of team 2's line call out the name of the person on the right end of team 1's line and repeat the process as before. Continue play everyone from one team has been captured by the other team or until it's obvious that everyone knows everyone else's name.

Teammates may not help each other name persons from the other team. Anyone who does must immediately go to the left end of the other team's line.

# ONE WORD

**NUMBER OF PLAYERS:** Any number

**LOCATION:** Anywhere

**THE GAME:** Form pairs. Have pairs sit on the floor and talk to each other by speaking one-word messages back and forth. Suggest one of the following topics for their one-word-at-a-time discussions:
- a recently solved problem,
- a favorite food,
- a favorite professional sports team,
- a fear,
- a dream, or
- a recent accomplishment.

Allow time for discussion, then use the following questions to further explore the value of communication. Ask:
- **What does this activity tell you about communication?**
- **How did you communicate without words?**
- **Read John 1:1-9. How did God communicate to us through Jesus Christ?**

# OPPOSITES ATTRACT

**NUMBER OF PLAYERS:** Any number

**LOCATION:** Anywhere

**THE GAME:** Form pairs of people who don't know each other. Then have kids identify two skills, hobbies, or interests their partners have that they don't. Then have partners introduce each other to the group by describing or pantomiming those skills.

# SNOOPING

**NUMBER OF PLAYERS:** Any number

**LOCATION:** Anywhere

**THE GAME:** Form pairs. Have partners talk about times they explored hidden or out-of-the-way places such as a cave, a hidden room, an attic, or a secret hiding place. Then have each student introduce his or her partner by leading the rest of the group in a game of 20 Questions to determine that person's secret place.

# TRADING PLACES

**NUMBER OF PLAYERS:** Any number

**LOCATION:** Anywhere

**THE GAME:** Form pairs of people who don't know each other well. Then have partners share the three or four most exciting things they've done in their lives. After kids tell their stories, have partners each choose one or two experiences that the other partner described that they wish they could experience, too. Then ask teenagers to introduce their partners to the entire group, describe those experiences, and explain why they would like to experience them, too.

# TRAVEL REPORT

**NUMBER OF PLAYERS:** Any number

**LOCATION:** Anywhere

**THE GAME:** Explain to your group members that they are travel writers. Ask them to introduce themselves and tell the group where in their travels they've encountered one or two of the following categories:

- worst food,
- noisiest hotel room,
- most reckless driver,
- best rest stop,
- worst restroom,
- friendliest people,
- scariest neighborhood,
- best junk food,
- biggest crowd,
- most unusual restaurant, or
- most memorable stranger.

# Ups and Downs

**NUMBER OF PLAYERS:** Any number

**LOCATION:** Anywhere

**THE GAME:** Use this activity to quickly introduce regular group members to new members. Ask regular group members to take a moment to reflect on what has happened to them since your last meeting. Then ask each person to say his or her name and describe the high point and low point during that time.

Ask kids to stand and speak in animated, excited voices when they describe the high moments and sit and speak in low, monotones when they describe the low moments.

# Weather Report

**NUMBER OF PLAYERS:** Any number

**LOCATION:** Anywhere

**THE GAME:** This activity works well when you ask strangers to introduce themselves to each other. Have them also report on two or three of the following topics. Tell teenagers that every answer they give must be from personal experience. Have group members describe

- the hottest temperature they've experienced,
- the coldest temperature they've experienced,
- the deepest snowfall they've seen,
- the worst windstorm they've experienced,
- the closest they've been to a tornado or hurricane,
- the densest fog they've witnessed,
- the most beautiful sunset they've seen, or
- the strangest weather they've experienced.

This is also a good crowdbreaker to use at events or meetings that have been forced inside by inclement weather!

## A-Z Travel Agency Race

**NUMBER OF PLAYERS:** 15 or more

**LOCATION:** Anywhere

**THE GAME:** Have kids form pairs. Tell partners to introduce themselves and tell each other about a place they have been that starts with the letter A. After pairs have shared, have kids form new pairs and repeat the process with the letter B. Instruct kids to keep forming new pairs and repeating the process until they reach Z. (To keep the game moving, allow kids a little freedom and flexibility with Q and X.)

If there are fewer than 26 people playing the game, kids will introduce themselves to the same people more than once. Players must sit down after they finish Z. The object of the game is to avoid being the last one seated. For an added incentive to make this game move quickly, let kids know ahead of time that the last two people seated will have to repeat the names and places visited by five of the people they introduced themselves to.

## At the Mall

**NUMBER OF PLAYERS:** Eight or more

**LOCATION:** Anywhere

**THE GAME:** Have group members imagine that they are at an unusual mall in which the stores sell experiences rather than

*Ready for more fun and relationship building? The games and crowd-breakers in this chapter go beyond "Hi! What's your name?" They help kids build deeper friendships through creative sharing and interaction.*

things. Tell kids they'll be able to browse at this mall but not buy. Then explain that each person in the room is a "store" and that each person's unique experiences are the merchandise.

During each round of play, have kids mill around, pretending to be the type of store you name, as they ask and answer the question associated with that type of store. Set a time limit for kids to visit each type of "store," then ask the group members to tell about their discoveries. Play as many rounds as necessary to help kids break the ice and become better acquainted.

- **A travel store: Who has traveled the greatest distance from home?**
- **A bedding store: Who has been away from home the most nights in the last year?**
- **A stationery store: Who writes the most letters in a year?**
- **A food store: Who has eaten the most unusual food?**
- **A pet store: Who has owned the most unusual pet?**
- **A clothing store: Who has worn the greatest number of different uniforms or costumes?**
- **A book store: Who has read the longest book, and what was it?**
- **A hobby store: Who has the same hobbies as you?**
- **A real estate office: Who has lived in the most number of houses, and who has lived in the least number of houses?**
- **An ice cream shop: What's the most popular flavor of ice cream?**
- **A music store: Whose taste in music is the same as yours?**
- **A cooking store: Who has cooked the most unusual food?**
- **A sporting goods store: Who has played in a sport or recreational activity that you haven't?**

# CLAN AND TRIBE

**NUMBER OF PLAYERS:** 15 or more

**LOCATION:** Anywhere

**THE GAME:** Tell kids that they are going to form different groups or "clans." Ask group members to choose from the following list the animal they most identify with. Instruct kids to keep their choices secret. After everyone has chosen a clan, have group members walk around silently shaking hands with everyone else in the room. Each person should shake the number of times specified by his or her clan. Have kids continue shaking hands until they've grouped themselves according to their clans.

Name enough clans to form small groups of five to nine members each. For example, if you have 25 kids, name only five clans from the following list.

- Bear Clan: one shake
- Turtle Clan: two shakes
- Wolf Clan: three shakes
- Raven Clan: four shakes
- Badger Clan: five shakes
- Rabbit Clan: six shakes
- Raccoon Clan: seven shakes
- Bobcat Clan: eight shakes
- Hawk Clan: nine shakes
- Fox Clan: 10 shakes

Then have kids follow the instructions for the five rounds of play described below.

**Round 1:** After group members are in their clans, direct them to introduce themselves. Then have each member tell about one beautiful place he or she has seen in the world.

**Round 2:** Choose one clan to be the chief clan. Instruct the members of this clan to make sure that every clan has an equal (or nearly equal) number of members. After the chief clan has evened up the clans, ask everyone to talk in their clans about places they have had to say good-bye to in their lives.

**Round 3:** Direct each clan to trade one clan member for a member of another clan. Then have the traded clan members ask their new clans three questions. For example, kids may ask about hobbies, interests, or favorite foods.

**Round 4:** Instruct each clan to trade two clan members for

two members of another clan. Then have the old members of each clan ask the new clan members three questions.

**Round 5:** Gather the clans together and have kids share new things they learned about each other through this activity.

# Exciting-Life Awards

**NUMBER OF PLAYERS:** Six or more

**LOCATION:** Anywhere

**THE GAME:** Form pairs and have partners introduce themselves. Then direct partners to tell each other one true story from the first category listed at the end of this activity.

After pairs are finished, have kids choose new partners and share stories from the second category. Continue until kids have talked with nine different partners about nine different things. If you have fewer than 10 kids, use fewer categories or have kids talk with the same partner about more than one category.

After kids finish the categories, gather the group and have kids introduce themselves. Then ask kids to nominate people for awards from any of the categories. Ask kids to explain why they chose to nominate these people by summarizing the stories they heard in their pair discussions. Continue until each person has been nominated at least once. (You many need to tell kids that this is one of the goals of the activity.) After the nominations have ceased, tell kids to give each other a standing ovation for living such exciting lives.

● Best Drama in Real Life (the most dramatic thing to happen in your life)

● Best Comedy Situation (the funniest thing that's happened to you)

● Best Horror Show (the scariest thing that's happened in your life)

● Best Mystery (the most mysterious thing you've experienced)

● Best Sporting Event (the most exciting athletic achievement you've either witnessed or participated in)

● Best News Coverage (the closest you've come to being an

eyewitness of a news story)

● Best Nature Special (the most beautiful experience you've had in nature)

● Best Musical Performance (the best musical performance you've experienced)

● Best Travel Show (the most interesting place you've been)

# GEOMETRY DRILL

**NUMBER OF PLAYERS:** 10 or more

**LOCATION:** Any room or open space large enough for your group to stand in a circle

**THE GAME:** This crowdbreaker will help group members understand what it takes to lead a group. It will also give kids a chance to get to know each other better by seeing how each person takes charge.

Explain that everyone in the group will take a turn leading the group through (and participating in) a simple drill step.

Your job, as the Game Master, is to give instructions to each person about what his or her leadership task is and to determine when that task has been accomplished so you can move to the next person in the circle.

Read the first instruction listed on page 29 to the first leader. If he or she has trouble understanding the instruction, explain to him or her only that step of the drill. Repeat the process for each leader. After each step, have the group members hold their place until the next leader gives them instructions. If you run out of leaders, start over again and have them lead another portion of the drill.

## INSTRUCTIONS FOR GEOMETRY DRILL

1. Lead everyone in standing in a perfect circle.
2. Lead everyone in standing in a single, perfectly straight line.
3. Lead everyone in standing in an equilateral (equal-sided) triangle.
4. Lead everyone in standing in a square.
5. Lead everyone in standing in a pentagon (five sides).
6. Lead everyone in standing in a five-pointed star.
7. Lead everyone in standing in a perfect circle again.
8. Lead everyone in clapping hands all at once.
9. Lead everyone in clapping once, then in the formation a single straight line.
10. Lead everyone in clapping twice, then in the formation of an equilateral triangle.
11. Lead everyone in clapping three times, then in the formation of a square.
12. Lead everyone in clapping four times, then in the formation of a pentagon.
13. Lead everyone in clapping five times, then in the formation of a five-pointed star.
14. Lead everyone in clapping six times, then in the formation of a circle again.
15. Lead everyone in doing all of the claps and all of the figure changes they just learned without a single interruption for instructions.
16. Lead everyone in a round of applause, then announce that this geometry dance is over.

After the crowdbreaker, use the following questions to help kids explore the nature of leadership. Ask:

● **What was frustrating about this activity?**
● **How easy is it to lead others?**
● **Read 1 Corinthians 9:19-23. How important is it for a leader to adapt to the needs of the group?**

# GET LOST

**NUMBER OF PLAYERS:** 12 or more (If you have fewer than 12 kids, use pairs instead of trios.)

**LOCATION:** Anywhere

**THE GAME:** Form trios and have kids introduce themselves. Then tell trio members to alphabetize their first names and make the person with the name closest to A "get lost." These people must quickly join different pairs. The last person to reach a different pair and the kids in that pair are eliminated from the game. Then instruct the new trio members to introduce themselves and tell each other when they were born. Direct the oldest and the youngest trio members to tell the other member to "get lost." As before, new trios are formed and three players are eliminated.

Continue to play with new criteria for getting lost until only one trio survives. For example, tell each trio to send away the person who

- has the most colorful socks,
- has the oldest living grandparent,
- has the most cousins,
- has the least pets, or
- owns the largest pet.

# GIFTS FOR THE JOURNEY

**NUMBER OF PLAYERS:** Eight or more

**LOCATION:** Anywhere

**THE GAME:** Form pairs. Say: **Imagine that you're going on a long journey and that you'll need lots of supplies. Now introduce yourself to your partner and describe one of your own possessions that you'd like to give to your partner to help on his or her journey. (Don't worry, you won't actually have to give up this item.)**

Explain that the gift can be either tangible (a Chicago Bulls team jacket, for example) or intangible (courage, for example).

After pairs finish, have kids find new partners, introduce themselves, and describe the gifts they received from their previous partners. Anyone who can't remember either the name or the gift is eliminated from the game. Then have partners exchange gifts as in the first round.

After pairs finish, form new pairs (and a trio, each time there is an uneven number of remaining players). But this time, teenagers must repeat the names and gifts of their two previous partners. Continue until three or fewer people are left.

# HIDDEN DIAMOND

**NUMBER OF PLAYERS:** Three or more

**LOCATION:** Anywhere

**THE GAME:** This game is a variation of Hide and Seek that helps kids learn about each other in a fun way.

Have each teenager take a turn mentally "hiding" the world's most valuable diamond somewhere in his or her favorite room at home. Kids can hide it anywhere that it would actually fit, such as in a box of cookies, under a computer table, or in an old sock. After someone hides the diamond, have him or her whisper the location to you or another appointed leader. Then let other group members take turns asking yes or no questions in order to determine the diamond's location. If, after 10 questions, no one discovers the diamond's location, declare the person who hid the diamond the winner and have him or her reveal the location. Continue play until everyone has had a turn hiding the diamond.

# I NEVER

**NUMBER OF PLAYERS:** Five or more

**LOCATION:** Anywhere

SUPPLIES · NO · REQUIRED

**THE GAME:** Instruct kids to form a circle. Place a leader in the center of the circle, ready to be tagged. The object of this game is to be the first person from the circle to tag the leader. However, kids may leave the circle to tag the leader only if the statement being read is absolutely true about them. After kids tag the leader, have them quickly return to the circle and await another opportunity to mob the leader.

Choose from the "I have never" statements on this and the following page (or come up with some of your own).

---

### I HAVE NEVER...

- I have never gone to Disneyland.
- I have never had my tonsils taken out.
- I have never driven a car.
- I have never pitched in a ballgame.
- I have never worn pink underwear.
- I have never been in a guys locker room.
- I have never lifted 100 pounds or more.
- I have never been to the Grand Canyon.
- I have never visited Aspen, Colorado.
- I have never played Monopoly.
- I have never worn a watch.
- I have never been to a slumber party.
- I have never seen *The Wizard of Oz*.
- I have never been sent to the principal's office.
- I have never attended my school's football games.
- I have never toured the state capitol building.
- I have never eaten junk food.
- I have never been on a "snipe" hunt.
- I have never had a brother.
- I have never had a sister.
- I have never toured the White House.
- I have never bought a meal at McDonald's.
- I have never eaten a taco.
- I have never owned a pet.
- I have never used an outhouse.
- I have never eaten spinach.

- I have never bought my own gum.
- I have never ridden in a Ford.
- I have never listened to country and western music on purpose.
- I have never watched MTV.
- I have never shoveled snow.

# I SURE HAVE!

**NUMBER OF PLAYERS:** Five or more

**LOCATION:** Anywhere

**THE GAME:** This is a variation of the previous game, I Never. Form a circle and have a leader stand in the center. As before, kids are to race to tag the leader if the statement you read is true of them. However, in this game the first person to tag the leader gets 1 point and must briefly describe the experience or item.

Read the following statements or make up some of your own.

## I HAVE...

- I have visited Walt Disney World.
- I have been caught stealing.
- I have posters on my bedroom wall.
- I have a pet dog.
- I have been to Yellowstone National Park.
- I have a pet bird.
- I have had an operation.
- I have wrecked on a bike.
- I have ridden a horse.
- I have a stuffed toy.
- I have been lost at the mall.
- I was born in another country.
- I have a video game system.
- I am the youngest child in my family.
- I have played on a soccer team.
- I was born someplace other than in a hospital.

- I have had my tonsils taken out.
- I have flown in an airplane more than twice.
- I play a musical instrument.
- I liked first grade.
- I have broken my arm or leg.
- I have climbed a mountain.

# IF I WERE . . .

**NUMBER OF PLAYERS:** Any number

**LOCATION:** Anywhere

**THE GAME:** Form pairs and read aloud one of the sentence completions from the list below. Then instruct partners to complete the sentence and explain their sentence completions to each other. After pairs finish, have kids choose new partners and complete a different sentence. Continue until each person has paired up with everyone else in the group at least once.

### IF I WERE...

- If I were an animal, I'd be...
- If I were a country, I'd be...
- If I were a racehorse, my name would be...
- If I were a season, I'd be...
- If I were a piece of furniture, I'd be...
- If I were a time of day, I'd be...
- If I were a movie star, the movie I'd win an Oscar for would be...
- If I were a writer, my best-selling book would be...
- If I were a prisoner, my crime would be...
- If I were an insect, I'd be...
- If I were a song, my title would be...
- If I were rich, I'd give a million dollars to...
- If I were dying, the reason would be...
- If I were a salesperson, I'd be selling...

- If I were a natural disaster, I'd be...
- If I were a hero, my claim to fame would be...
- If I were a teacher, I'd teach...

# WHERE WERE YOU?

**NUMBER OF PLAYERS:** Five or more

**LOCATION:** Anywhere

**THE GAME:** Have group members sit in a circle. Then choose one person to be the Chief Inspector and instruct that person to stand in the center of the circle. Then direct the Chief Inspector to go to someone in the circle and ask that person where he or she was on a specific day during the last two weeks, a specific month in the last year, or a specific year in his or her life. For example, the Chief Inspector might ask, "Where were you last Tuesday night?" or "Where were you last December?" or "Where were you at age 5?"

Allow the person to answer the question honestly or dishonestly, then have the Chief Inspector guess whether the answer is true or false. If the Chief Inspector guesses correctly, the person who answered the question becomes the new Chief Inspector. Continue until each person in the circle has been questioned at least once.

# BODY SPELLER

**NUMBER OF PLAYERS:** Four or more

**LOCATION:** Anywhere

**THE GAME:** Form two or more teams. Then have team members take turns standing in front of their teams and spelling out words or phrases for the other team members to guess. Tell kids that they are not allowed to talk or mouth the words. You'll assign various methods that kids can use to spell the words.

For example, you might have the first spellers use only their index fingers to write the word or phrase in the air and the second spellers use only their feet to spell the words. Be creative in your choice of methods. Have kids spell words with their elbows, knees, heads, and (if you're really adventurous) hips.

Award a point to the first team to correctly identify each word or phrase. Total each team's points at the end of the activity and have everyone else give the winning team a standing ovation.

The words and phrases listed below will help you get things started. Use 10 or so from the list or think up your own.

- high school
- rock and roll
- salamander
- wishes
- elephant
- salad
- nightmare
- Saturn
- west
- wind
- abracadabra
- chase
- Bugs Bunny
- cautiously

# GAMES

*This chapter includes a wide range of fun and challenging activities to be played indoors. You'll find everything from thought-provoking, serious games to out-of-this-world, insane games. In this chapter, you'll find something for every group's mood from quiet to loud, high energy to deep concentration.*

- Englishwoman
- Timbuktu
- smash hit
- such silliness
- tarantula
- rainy day

- understood
- shallow
- perspiration
- delicious
- goose bumps

# CATERPILLAR RACE

**NUMBER OF PLAYERS:** Six or more

**LOCATION:** Anywhere

**THE GAME:** Form teams of equal size, with five to seven players on each team. (If you have a small group, teams of three also work well.) Have kids think up one-syllable names for their teams. Then line teams up next to each other behind a starting line. Instruct team members to place their hands on the shoulders of the team members in front of them and race to a finish line according to the following rules of movement.

- The first person in line may hop one step forward. Then the next person in line may hop one step forward. Continue down the line until the last person in line hops one step forward. After the last person hops, he or she must shout the team name. Then the whole team may hop one step forward at the same time. Repeat this process to move the caterpillar along.

- Players must keep their hands on the shoulders of the team members in front of them at all times during the race.

● Players may move forward only by hopping one step forward with both feet at once.

● If a team breaks any of the above rules, it must return to the starting line and begin again.

# DISCERNMENT

**NUMBER OF PLAYERS:** Any number

**LOCATION:** Anywhere

**THE GAME:** Form pairs of group members who don't know each other well. Ask teenagers to take turns telling their partners one true and one false story about their childhoods. Have partners guess which story is true and which isn't. Then have kids find new partners and repeat the process.

For extra fun, have kids keep track of the number of times they guessed correctly during the game. Have the person with the most correct guesses share with the whole group his or her secrets for discerning truth.

# EQUILIBRIUM

**NUMBER OF PLAYERS:** Three or more

**LOCATION:** Anywhere

**THE GAME:** Form three teams: A, B, and C. The game is played in turns. Each turn, teams A and B each secretly choose a number between one and three. Team C, however, secretly assigns two numbers (one and two, one and three, or two and three) to either team A or team B and the remaining number to the other team.

After teams choose numbers, representatives from the teams tell the leader their teams' choices. Using the chart on page 39, the leader determines whether team A wins, team B wins, or they tie, which means that team C wins.

The key to the game is that teams A and B win a point only if they don't pick a number team C assigns them. If, after 10 rounds (or as many as you set ahead of time), teams A and B are tied, team C wins. Otherwise, the team with the highest score wins.

Since the team that is assigned two numbers is less likely to win, team C may attempt to keep teams A and B tied by assigning the leading team two numbers. After a few rounds, kids will begin to work out strategies for outsmarting each other.

| TEAM C ASSIGNS TO → | | A | B | A | B | A | B | A | B | A | B | A | B |
|---|---|---|---|---|---|---|---|---|---|---|---|---|---|
| **TEAM A PICKS:** | **TEAM B PICKS:** | 1 | 2,3 | 2 | 1,3 | 3 | 1,2 | 1,2 | 3 | 1,3 | 2 | 2,3 | 1 |
| 1 | 1 | B wins | | A wins | | A wins | | B wins | | B wins | | A wins | |
| 1 | 2 | Tie | | Tie | | A wins | | B wins | | Tie | | Tie | |
| 1 | 3 | Tie | | A wins | | Tie | | Tie | | B wins | | Tie | |
| 2 | 1 | Tie | | Tie | | A wins | | B wins | | Tie | | Tie | |
| 2 | 2 | A wins | | B wins | | A wins | | B wins | | A wins | | B wins | |
| 2 | 3 | A wins | | Tie | | Tie | | Tie | | Tie | | B wins | |
| 3 | 1 | Tie | | A wins | | Tie | | Tie | | B wins | | Tie | |
| 3 | 2 | A wins | | Tie | | Tie | | Tie | | Tie | | B wins | |
| 3 | 3 | A wins | | A wins | | B wins | | A wins | | B wins | | B wins | |

# Fists and Fingers

**NUMBER OF PLAYERS:** Any number

**LOCATION:** Anywhere

**THE GAME:** These four variations of the same game require quick thinking and may frustrate kids at first. With practice, your group will become expert at even the most difficult version of the game.

This game is easiest when played in trios, with each trio member taking a turn as the referee for the other two members. The referee is responsible for determining the correct response and who said it first. Because of its difficulty, you might want to reserve the "Impossible" variation for the final rounds of an elimination tournament.

**Easy:** Form pairs. Have partners stand, face each other, and put their hands behind their backs. Then have each partner hold out between zero and 10 fingers without letting the other partner see. On your signal, players must quickly show how many fingers they are holding out. The first partner to call out the correct number of fingers showing on all four hands (that's both partners') wins the round. Repeat until one partner wins two out of three rounds.

**Difficult:** As in the "Easy" variation, have partners face each other and hold their hands behind their backs. However, this time players need to decide whether to show either or both hands as fists or either or both with all five fingers held out. On your signal, kids must quickly show their hands. The first partner to say the correct word for the number of fists showing wins the round. The words assigned to the number of fists are listed below.

- zero fists: strawberry
- one fist: pie
- two fists: fruit
- three fists: apple
- four fists: red

Play until one partner wins two out of three rounds.

**Really Tough:** If possible, play this version immediately after the "Difficult" variation. As before, have partners face each other and hold their hands behind their backs. Then have each partner hold out between zero and five fingers on one hand. On your signal, have partners quickly show how many fingers they are holding out. The first player to say the correct word for the total number of fingers on both players' hands wins the round. The words assigned to the number of fingers are listed below.

- zero fingers: cherry
- one or two fingers: green
- three or four fingers: fruit
- five or six fingers: gooseberry
- seven or eight fingers: apple
- nine or 10 fingers: pie

Play until one partner wins two out of three rounds.

**Impossible:** When players have mastered the first three variations, play the "Easy" variation again. However, instead of calling
out the total number of fingers on all four hands, kids must call
out words that match the number of fingers held out.

- zero fingers: raspberry
- one or two fingers: green
- three or four fingers: orange
- five or six fingers: grapefruit
- seven or eight fingers: fruit
- nine or 10 fingers: chokecherry
- 11 or 12 fingers: cake
- 13 or 14 fingers: red
- 15 or 16 fingers: cucumber
- 17 or 18 fingers: apple
- 19 or 20 fingers: pie

Once again, play until one partner wins two out of three
rounds.

Use the following questions to spark discussion after this
game. Ask:

- **What are your reactions to this game?**
- **Generally, teenagers are better at this game than
adults. Why do you think this is so?**
- **Read 1 Timothy 4:12. What are some of the confusing
issues you as a young person deal with?**
- **How can you be an example to others with your
words? actions? love? faith? pure life?**

# GAME CHEST

**NUMBER OF PLAYERS:** Any number

**LOCATION:** Anywhere

**THE GAME:** Here's a grab bag of partner games to use any time.

**Blink:** Two partners stare into each other's eyes. The first to
blink loses.

**Hand Slap:** One partner holds out his or her hands palms up
while the other partner places his or her hands palms down on

top of them. Partners should maintain palm-to-palm contact until the "bottom" partner moves either of his or her hands. The object of the game is for the partner whose hands are on the bottom to slap the tops of his or her partner's hands before that partner can withdraw them. Partners switch roles after each attempt.

**Monkey See, Monkey Do:** Two partners stand several feet apart and face each other. Each takes a turn being the leader. Both start with their hands at their sides. The leader then quickly raises both hands overhead or simply raises forearms and points at his or her partner. The instant the leader moves, the other partner must copy his or her actions. If the leader's movement is copied by the partner, the partner wins. If the leader's movement is not copied by the partner, the leader wins.

**Off Balance:** Two partners stand toe to toe. Then they clasp hands so that their fingers are woven together.
　　On your signal, partners attempt to push or pull each other off balance. The first person to move his or her foot loses the round.

**Push and Pull:** Two partners place their right feet, pointing in opposite directions, side by side and touching each other. Then they shake right hands, grasping each other's thumbs.
　　On your signal, partners try to pull or push each other off balance using only their right arms. Whoever moves his or her feet to maintain balance loses the round. After someone wins, repeat the game using left feet and left hands.

　　For added fun, try this group variation of the games in the "Game Chest" collection.
　　**Attrition:** Form pairs. Then form two lines, with partners facing each other. On your signal, have pairs play two rounds of one of the partner games above. If both partners win one round each,

nothing changes and both remain for the second round. But if one partner wins both rounds, the losing partner is out the game. Winning partners then join new partners from the opposite line to play the next two rounds. If one side has more partners than the other, the extra player must wait until there are enough partners on the other side for him or her to pair with.

The object of this variation is to eliminate the members of the other line. For more laughs, have kids who lose act out dramatic death scenes when they leave their lines.

# GENIUS

**NUMBER OF PLAYERS:** Six to nine per group (Many small groups can play simultaneously.)

**LOCATION:** Anywhere

**THE GAME:** Have everyone in the group except for one person form a circle. The person outside the circle is the Genius. Have circle members reach into the circle and grab the hands of two different people, one with each of hand. Tell kids that they can't grab the hands of either person immediately beside them.

Once everyone is holding hands, no one in the circle may speak. Circle members must, however, follow any reasonable instructions given by the Genius. It's the Genius' job to give instructions that will untangle the circle members so they form an untangled circle. (Sometimes two circles are formed.) However, kids may not release each other's hands in the process.

Keep track of the number of instructions it takes the Genius to untangle the circle. Then choose a new Genius and try again. The winner is the Genius who uses the fewest instructions to untangle the circle.

# GIVE ME 10

**NUMBER OF PLAYERS:** Eight or more

**LOCATION:** Anywhere

**THE GAME:** Choose one person to be the Slapper. Have the others sit in chairs in a circle and put their hands on their knees, palms up. To start the game, instruct the Slapper to walk around inside the circle and slap both hands of another player then quickly slap the hands of another player. After the Slapper slaps the second person's hands, the first person slapped is to get up, slap the second person's hands, and try to tag the Slapper before the Slapper sits in the first person's vacated chair.

If the Slapper makes it to the chair before being tagged, he or she wins and the person standing becomes the Slapper for the next round. If the Slapper is tagged, he or she remains the Slapper for another round. Play until kids get tired of racing around the circle (or until just before their hands start to hurt!).

# HOT-HANDS RELAY

**NUMBER OF PLAYERS:** Eight or more

**LOCATION:** Any room large enough to run relays in

**THE GAME:** Form teams of four or eight. Send half of each team to opposite sides of the room. Then explain that kids will be running a basic relay race. However, instead of simply tagging teammates, the persons running must create original hand or arm signs that other team members must imitate before running their legs of the race.

For example, after the first player runs, he or she is to create a hand or arm sign, which the second runner must imitate before starting the second leg of the race. After running the second leg, the second runner must use the first sign and add another original sign. The third runner must repeat the two signs before running. Each time a runner tags someone else to run, he or she must add a new sign (always after repeating the other signs first). If any player forgets the sign sequence, his or her team must begin the race again.

The team that finishes first wins. After the race, have groups demonstrate their sign sequences for each other. Use the following questions to spark discussion after the game.

- **How did you feel frustrated and pressured in this game?**
- **What are some of the frustrations and pressures you face in your life?**
- **What pressures do we put on each other that lead to frustration?**
- **Read Matthew 11:28-30. How can God provide relief from pressure and frustration?**

# HUMAN CHECKERS

**NUMBER OF PLAYERS:** Six or more

**LOCATION:** A square room wide enough for half of your group members to stand in a line with arms out, fingertip to fingertip

**THE GAME:** Form two teams and have each team choose a captain. The captain should know every player on the team by name. To begin play, instruct the two teams to line up on opposite sides of the play area. Direct the captains to stay behind or stand off to the side. Determine which team gets to go first.

Instruct the captain of the first team to call out the name of any member of his or her team. This player must then take a single step forward toward the other team. Then the captain of the other team is to call out the name of a member of his or her team, and that person must take a step toward the opposition. Continue play by alternating back and forth between teams. However, a captain may not call the same person's name two turns in a row.

Players are eliminated from the game in two ways. First, any player who takes more than one step, steps to the side, or loses his or her balance is eliminated from the game. Second, if during a player's turn (after taking a step and before the next player is called) that player reaches out and successfully tags an opposing team member, the tagged player is eliminated.

Players who reach the other end of the room without being tagged remain in the game but may not be called by the captain again. When no one can move or all the members of one team have been eliminated, the game is over. The winning team is the one with the most survivors at the end of the game.

# INDIANAPOLIS 5

**NUMBER OF PLAYERS:** 10 or more

**LOCATION:** Any large, unobstructed area

**THE GAME:** Form teams of five to seven players. Mark out a circular racecourse. Say: **The object of this game is to be the fastest team to run five laps around our track. But you must carry a different team member each lap. After each lap you must stop, choose a new person to carry, then carry that person around the course. We'll keep track of how long each team takes to complete the course, and the fastest time wins.**

At least three people must carry the team member each lap. Extra team members can wait by the starting line and replace carriers as necessary on the next lap. To carry a team member, two players create a "seat" by facing each other and grasping arms together. The person being carried then sits or lies back into this seat, and the third carrier grabs his or her feet.

Time the teams to determine which is the fastest. If your room is large enough, you may want to have two teams race at the same time.

# KING OF THE JUNGLE

**NUMBER OF PLAYERS:** Eight or more

**LOCATION:** Any area large enough for everyone to sit in a circle

**THE GAME:** Form a circle, making sure everyone in the circle can see everyone else. Assign someone to be the Lion. The person to the left of the Lion is the Elephant and the last in line. Then assign everyone else in the circle an animal from the list below and on page 48. After you assign kids their animals, have them practice the hand signals for their animals.

The object of this game is to be the Lion when play runs out. To start play, instruct the Lion to make his or her sign and to immediately follow that sign with the sign of another animal. That animal must then make his or her sign and any other animal's sign. Play continues this way until someone makes a mistake.

When someone makes a mistake, he or she may have to trade places with another person in the circle. If the person who made the mistake is closer in rank to the Lion than the last person to make a sign correctly, those two players must switch places and trade animals. If the person who made the mistake is farther from the Lion, there is no change and the Lion restarts play.

Unlike other players, the Lion cannot repeat an animal sign (other than his or her own) in a round. In other words, any time the Lion makes another animal's sign, it must be one that he or she hasn't yet made during that round. If the Lion makes a mistake and repeats an animal sign, the person whose sign was copied gets to trade places with the Lion. To keep track of which animals the Lion has called, you may want to instruct the called animals to cross their legs or give some other simple sign.

- Lion: Raise your arms around your head to form a mane.
- Pig: Push the tip of your nose up with your index finger.
- Elephant: Raise one arm horizontally in front of you to create a trunk; use the other arm to form a large ear on the side of your head.
- Bat: Create "glasses" by connecting thumbs and forefingers, then flip the glasses so remaining fingers are facing down.
- Coyote: Raise your hand high, then quickly drop it to the floor.
- Roadrunner: Spin your hands around each other in front of you, then quickly send one straight out in front of you.
- Dragon: Create fists with index fingers out, then point to

your nostrils.

● Blowfish: Puff your cheeks and place your hands by the side of your face as fins.

● Gorilla: Beat your chest.

● Mouse: Place your fists on your head as ears.

● Giraffe: Raise one arm above your head, make a fist, and bend it down at the wrist.

● Monkey: Pretend to pick bugs off a neighbor...then eat them.

● Rooster: Open your palm as a comb above your forehead.

● Anteater: Stretch out your arms in front of you, put your hands together, place your head between your arms, and bend down.

● Cat: Use two fingers of each hand to make whiskers on each side of your head.

● Dog: Make a sniffing sound.

● Pronghorn: Use your index fingers to make horns protruding from your forehead.

● Lizard: Stick out your tongue in lizardlike fashion.

● Spider: Use one hand as a spider to climb up your other arm.

● Fly: Move your finger crazily through air.

● Chimpanzee: Scratch under your arm.

● Trout: Hold your palms together and move forward in a graceful, fishlike swimming motion.

● Horse: Show your teeth and raise your head.

● Duck: Place your hands in front of your mouth as a bill and move them as though you are quacking.

● Inchworm: Inch an index finger forward on your arm.

● Eagle: Make wide flapping motions with your arms.

● Rabbit: Hold up two fingers behind your head.

● Alligator: Hold your arms straight in front of you, then loudly clap them together.

● Goldfish: Pinch your lips together in a pucker.

● Skunk: Pinch your nose closed.

● Penguin: Tuck your thumbs under your armpits and flap your arms.

● Koala: Hug the person next to you.

● Moose: Place your thumbs at the side of your head with your fingers splayed out like antlers.

# MURDER MYSTERY

**NUMBER OF PLAYERS:** This game works best with 12 or more players, but it can be used with just the six players needed to be suspects.

**LOCATION:** Anywhere

## THE GAME: This game can be played with groups competing against each other or by a single group. To start play, have kids imagine that a police detective and a number of police officers are waiting outside. Every now and then, step outside to "confer" with the detective.

Say: **A police detective claims that a number of our group members fit the description of a suspect wanted in the scandalous murder of Lady Chantel Hawkins, which took place four days ago. I asked the police detective for clues that would reveal which of our group members is the chief suspect in the murder. The detective and several police officers are waiting outside to arrest the guilty party as soon as we determine who this person is.**

**Would the following suspects please step forward?** (After a person is named as a suspect, he or she cannot be named a second time.)

● **Suspect One is the person born closest to January 13.**

● **Suspect Two is the person who has most recently visited** (or come closest to) **Yellowstone National Park.**

● **Suspect Three is the person who most recently visited** (or came closest to) **Disneyland or Walt Disney World.**

● **Suspect Four is the person who watched the least amount of television last week.**

● **Suspect Five is wearing** (name a unique article of clothing or piece of jewelry worn by a person you want to include in the game).

**Finally, Suspect Six is the shortest** (or tallest) **person still in the group.**

**Now we have our suspects. Before we move on to the next part of our meeting, I need the rest of the group to help me solve this mystery. Listen closely while I read the clues but don't be surprised if the things you hear about our suspects seem surprising. The police have made a thorough investigation, and at least one of the suspects is a master of disguise**

and deception. Unfortunately, the clues aren't well organized. You'll have to make sense of them as best you can.

In order to maintain the secrecy of their investigation, the police have provided me with only one set of clues. They ask that I read them to you. You may ask me to repeat any of the clues, but you may not write any of them down, and you may not see my written text. The police are very sure that these clues will identify the murderer.

Oh, and one more thing. When we identify the suspect, we also have to identify the weapon the suspect used and the location of the murder. If we don't, the police will not accept the results of our investigation.

After each clue, I'll report any conclusions you form to the police detective waiting outside. The detective will tell me if you're right or wrong.

These are the clues:

1. The police know that only one of five possible weapons was used in the murder: a chainsaw, a harpoon, a wooden mallet, a small revolver, or a piece of nylon cord.

2. There are only six places that the murder could have taken place: Redwood National Park; Nome, Alaska; Buckingham Palace; Cairo, Egypt; along the Great Wall of China; or Everglades National Park.

3. Only Suspect Five could have broken into Buckingham Palace to commit a murder there.

4. Suspect Four was in Nome, Alaska, when the murder occurred.

5. A chainsaw was the only lethal device found in Everglades National Park.

6. If the murder took place at Cairo, Egypt, Suspect One did it.

7. The only weapon Suspect Three had access to was a harpoon.

8. Suspect Two was in Redwood National Park at the time of the murder.

9. Suspect Four has never traveled to the Great Wall of China.

10. The American embassy in Egypt reports that police

in Cairo have witnesses who saw Suspect One there at the time of the murder.

11. Suspect Five owns a chainsaw.

12. Suspect Two was not with Suspect Three at the scene of the murder.

13. Suspects Five and Six were together at the time of the murder.

14. Only Suspect Two is known to have had access to a wooden mallet.

15. The only weapon found in the search of Nome, Alaska, was a small revolver.

16. Intensive analysis by the FBI shows that Suspect Six was the only one to handle the piece of nylon cord.

17. Suspect Six was in Everglades National Park when the murder occurred.

18. The weapon at Nome, Alaska, is an antique and could not be used at the time of the murder because of the cold weather.

19. Only one suspect was present at the murder.

20. The only weapon Suspect One could have killed anyone with was a piece of nylon cord.

21. Suspect Two did not do it.

(The answer to "Murder Mystery" may be found on page 94.)

# RED, WHITE, AND BLUE

**NUMBER OF PLAYERS:** Eight or more

**LOCATION:** Anywhere

**THE GAME:** Have each group member secretly choose one of the following colors: red, white, or blue. Tell group members that they can't change colors after they choose them. Then explain that red kills white, white kills blue, and blue kills red.

On your signal, have kids go around the room and take turns whispering their colors in each other's ears. If two people whisper the same color, they must move on to other partners. Any time red is whispered in a white's ear, white has to drop immediately to the ground and play dead until the game is over. Likewise, if white is whispered in a blue's ear, blue must fall down and play dead. If blue is whispered in a red's ear, red has to fall down and play dead. Players may not avoid each other in this game. They must seek out others and whisper their colors until the game is over. The game ends when only one color remains "alive." Those who chose that color are the winners.

# TEAM SLALOM

**NUMBER OF PLAYERS:** Any number

**LOCATION:** Anywhere

**THE GAME:** Form two teams. Have the members of each team form a circle with members standing sideways and an arm's length apart. Instruct team members to place their hands on the shoulders of the person in front of them, lean forward, and arch their backs to form bridges.

Then, on your signal, have a member of each team step out of the circle, weave in and out of all the bridges in the circle, and return to his or her original position. As soon as the first person returns, the next person in line may leave and slalom around the circle. Continue until everyone on the team has run through the slalom. The first team to finish wins.

# THE SECRET OF MY SUCCESS

**NUMBER OF PLAYERS:** Nine or more

**LOCATION:** Anywhere

**THE GAME:** Form trios. Then assign each trio a letter of the alphabet. Trio A will be the top group, trio B the second, and so forth.

The object of the game is to end as a member of trio A. Each turn, members of each trio will secretly decide which of four elements—Earth, Wind, Fire, or Water—the trio will be. Then they will assign one of the three principles listed for that element to each of the trio members. Finally, they'll rank the three principles in any order from 1 to 3.

| ELEMENTS AND PRINCIPLES | |
|---|---|
| **ELEMENT** | **PRINCIPLES** |
| Earth | Mountain, Valley, Plain |
| Wind | Tornado, Gust, Breeze |
| Fire | Sunlight, Earthlight, Moonlight |
| Water | Ocean, River, Creek |

Once trios have made their decisions, ask the last trio to whisper to you the name of its element and the order of the principles. Then go to the next highest trio and have its members whisper the same information to you.

Without revealing which elements or principles were chosen, read the following rules and switch players between the two trios according to the rules:

1. Players can be switched between trios only if the two trios pick the same element.

2. A member of a lower trio may move up only if the ranking of his or her principle matches the ranking of the same principle in the higher trio. So, for example, if the two groups both chose Earth and both ranked Mountain first, but differed on the ranking of Valley and Plain, only the lower trio member assigned Mountain would switch with his or her counterpart in the higher trio.

After making any possible switches between the bottom two trios, ask the third-to-last trio to whisper its element and order of principles. As before, without revealing this trio's choices, switch players between the second- and third-to-last trios. Continue this process until you have completed any possible switches between trios. End the game after a predetermined time and declare the final members of trio A the winners.

To speed play, you may want to assign each element a number from one to four. Then have each trio sit in a circle on the floor and ask one member of each trio to secretly indicate with fingers the number of the trio's element.

# THIS, THAT, AND THE OTHER

**NUMBER OF PLAYERS:** Any number

**LOCATION:** Any open area

**THE GAME:** These are variations of Paper, Scissors, Stone. Form pairs for each game.

**Cliff, Climber, Ground:** To keep kids from slugging each other, play this variation in a large area. Have partners stand facing away from each other, approximately three feet apart. On your signal they are to jump around, face each other, and assume one of three positions:
- cliff: arms held straight up
- climber: one fist on a hip, the other fist held out in front
- ground: both arms held straight out to the sides

If partners assume the same position, they tie and repeat the game. If partners are in different positions, determine the winner according to the following rules.
- Cliff beats ground (because it rises above it).
- Climber beats cliff (by climbing it).
- Ground beats climber (by squashing the climber after a fall).

**Eye Opener:** Tell partners to stand face to face with their eyes closed. On your signal, have partners open one or both eyes. If partners open the same eye or both open both eyes, they tie. If partners open different eyes, determine the winner according to the following rules.
- Left eye open beats right eye open.
- Right eye open beats both eyes open.
- Both eyes open beat left eye open.

**Knife, Fork, Spoon:** Instruct partners to stand face to face and hold their hands behind their backs. On your signal, have kids bring out a hand (either left or right) and hold it in one of three positions:

● knife: palm held vertically, fingers together

● fork: palm held down, fingers spread out

● spoon: palm held up, fingers forming a cup

If partners hold out the same hand in the same position, they tie and repeat the game. Anyone who mistakenly moves both hands automatically loses. Otherwise, the winner is determined by the following rules.

If partners bring out the same hand:
● knife beats fork.
● fork beats spoon.
● spoon beats knife.

If one player brings out a left hand and the other brings out a right hand:
● spoon beats fork.
● fork beats knife.
● knife beats spoon.

# ARCHITECTURE

**NUMBER OF PLAYERS:** Five or more

**LOCATION:** Anywhere with a soft landing surface (Grassy or sandy locations work best.)

**THE GAME:** Instead of having kids create human pyramids, have teams of up to 10 create other human structures and shapes. For example, a team could form a castle, a cathedral, a bank, a gas station, a fast-food restaurant, a stadium, a geyser, a local high school, a flock of geese, a mall, a waterfall, a sailing yacht, a parking lot, the Leaning Tower of Pisa, a locker room, a car, a local landmark, a tepee, a seashore with waves, a space shuttle, the solar system, a capitol dome, the Statue of Liberty, or a roller coaster.

Have a panel of impartial judges determine which sculpture is best. For extra fun, have kids create two sculptures and smoothly shift from one to the other.

# BAREHANDED BASEBALL

**NUMBER OF PLAYERS:** Nine or more

**LOCATION:** Any open field

**THE GAME:** Form two teams of at least four players each and select an umpire. If you have an extra player, have this person act as the scorekeeper. A basic understanding of baseball is required

# R GAMES

*When a beautiful day beckons, what's a youth leader to do? Take the kids outside, of course! So here are some great games to take with you. They range from "just for fun" games to "growing closer as a group" games, but all provide a great way to enjoy the weather together.*

for this game.

Set up one team in the field by placing a player beside each imaginary base: first, second, and third. Instruct a fourth player to stand on the imaginary pitcher's mound. Any extra players may stand in the outfield. In this version of baseball, every fielder gets a turn as the pitcher. Have the umpire stand behind home plate.

When someone comes up to bat, he or she is to turn away from the pitcher and face the umpire. Using the fingers on one hand, the batter should secretly indicate to the umpire a number between zero and five. The umpire, without revealing the batter's number, should then look to the pitcher, who will "throw" a pitch by signaling with his or her fingers a number between zero and five.

The umpire will then add the two numbers and announce the results of the pitch according to the following rules:

| | |
|---|---|
| 0 = Strike | 6 = Strike |
| 1 = Foul | 7 = Double |
| 2 = Ball | 8 = Ball |
| 3 = Single | 9 = Triple |
| 4 = Out | 10 = Strike |
| 5 = Home run | |

Have teams play three to nine innings. Remember to rotate fielders onto the pitcher's mound. To add drama, have kids act out the game as if they were playing a real game of baseball. Also, be sure to have plenty of imaginary popcorn to hawk to confused onlookers.

# EARTH, WIND, FIRE, AND WATER

**NUMBER OF PLAYERS:** 12 or more (If you have fewer than 12 in your group, this game may be played using fewer "elements.")

**LOCATION:** Any field in which your group can spread out and run around

**THE GAME:** Ask for four volunteers to start this game. Have everyone else spread out randomly on a playing field. Assign each of the four volunteers one of the following elements: Earth, Wind, Fire, and Water.

Say: **In this game, the four people representing elements are competing with each other; the rest of you are pawns. Each element will attempt to tag more people than the other. The winner is the element who has the most people on his or her side at the end of the game. When you're tagged, you must act like the element represented by the person who tagged you. For example, if you're tagged by Earth, you must crouch down in a ball, as though you are a rock. If you're tagged by Wind, you must fall to the ground and lie flat, as though you've been blown over. If you're tagged by Fire, you must sit down and shake your hands as though they're on fire. And if you're tagged by Water, you must kneel and hold up your arms to catch rain.**

Players who are not tagged may race around and free the tagged players by tagging them. After two to five minutes, stop play and determine which element is the winner. Then pick new people to be elements and play again.

# GRAND ELIMINATION

**NUMBER OF PLAYERS:** Eight or more (You need an even number of players for this game.)

**LOCATION:** Any open, level area where players can run

**THE GAME:** For the first round of this event, line up kids at a starting line. On your signal, have kids race to a predetermined finish line by running backward. Then have kids line up according to the order in which they finished, from first to last.

For round two, form pairs based on how players finished the first round. Pair the first-place runner with the last-place runner, the second-place runner with the second-to-last-place runner, and so on. Instruct pairs to stand back to back and to link elbows. On your signal, have pairs race to a finish line.

Form two teams for the final round. Have the pair that won the second round join the last-place pair to form the core of one team. Then form the second team's core by joining the second-place pair to the second-to-last-place pair. Continue in this manner until every pair has been assigned to a team. (If you have an uneven number of pairs, divide the middle pair between the two teams.)

Direct each team to stand in a circle facing out and link elbows. Then have the two circles race to a predetermined finish line. The team that crosses the line first wins.

After the game, use the following discussion questions to get kids thinking about competition. Ask:

- **How did the way you were paired affect your race?**
- **What does this game teach us about competition?**
- **Read Matthew 20:1-16. What does this passage tell us about how God ranks people in the race of life?**

# HUMAN HORSESHOES

**NUMBER OF PLAYERS:** Three or more

**LOCATION:** Any open area approximately the same size as a regular horseshoe playing area

**THE GAME:** For this game, kids will need to remove their shoes. Select the two largest shoes and place them at least 20 feet apart. Then have kids play Horseshoes by tossing their own shoes at the two "posts." Award 1 point for shoes that touch the posts, 2 points for shoes that lean against the posts, and 3 points for shoes that land on the posts and don't touch the ground. Play with teams of three or more and declare the team with the highest total score the winner.

# INVISIBLE BALL

**NUMBER OF PLAYERS:** Eight or more

**LOCATION:** Any large, open space

**THE GAME:** Form two teams and send them to opposite ends of a large, open space. Have the members of each team number off.

In each variation of this game, you'll call out random numbers while players with those numbers run to the center of the playing area. To keep things interesting, have kids trade numbers within their teams from time to time.

**Invisible-Ball Tag:** Mark a spot on the ground in the center of the field. (You can use a shoe if necessary.) Say: **There is an invisible ball on top of the center spot. The only way to pick up the invisible ball is to run to the spot and slap your hand on it. Once the invisible ball is picked up by a player, his or her opponent must try to tag the ball carrier before he or she gets back to tag a team member. Two points are awarded to a team if one of its players successfully brings the invisible ball back. One point is awarded to a team if one of its players tags the ball carrier.**

If both players' hands hit the center spot at the same time, declare a draw and award no points for that round. Explain that team members whose numbers aren't called must remain on their sides of the play area. Call out numbers at random and keep score. The team with the most points after a predetermined time limit wins the game.

**Invisible-Ball Relay:** This version is played just like Invisible-Ball Tag, except that the leader must call out two or more numbers at a time. Once again, the object is for players to grab the invisible ball and take it back to their teams. However, any opposing team member whose number has been called may tag the ball carrier. Also, the ball carrier may pass the ball by tagging a team member and saying "pass." Points are awarded the same way as in the first variation.

**Humorless Variation:** As before, call out a number and have opponents meet in the center of the playing area. Then these two players must attempt to get each other to smile by any means that doesn't involve touching. The first person to make his or her partner smile wins a point for his or her team.

# MESSENGER RELAY

**NUMBER OF PLAYERS:** Eight or more

**LOCATION:** Any space large enough for a large racetrack

**THE GAME:** Form equal teams of at least four players each. Explain that teams will compete in a relay race around the track. Place team members equal distances apart from each other around the track.

Say: **I'm going to whisper a phrase or sentence into the first runners' ears. On my signal, they must race to the second players and repeat the phrase before those people start their leg of the race. We continue this way until the last racers cross the finish line and whisper the phrase to me. If the first-place team's phrase is exactly correct, that team wins. If it's incorrect and the second-place team's is correct, the second-place team wins. If neither is correct, both teams lose.**

Use nonsensical phrases such as "The pig went shopping on Thursday in the rain" or "Seventy-five thunderstorms make for lots of lasagna." Have fun creating zany phrases and vary them each time you play.

This game is a great introduction to a group meeting on the importance of clear communication or on the dangers of being too busy to listen carefully to others.

# MOCKINGBIRDS

**NUMBER OF PLAYERS:** Six or more

**LOCATION:** Any grassy or sandy area large enough for your group to stand in a circle

## THE GAME:
Form a circle. Choose one person to be the Caller and have him or her stand in the middle of the circle. The Caller may point to any player in the circle and say, "Do this!" After saying this, the Caller must move in a certain way—roll on the ground three times, do a cartwheel or a somersault, or do five jumping jacks, for example. While the Caller is performing the action, the rest of the group is to count out loud. As soon as the Caller finishes, he or she must shout "done." Then the group must start counting again while the person the Caller pointed to attempts to repeat the Caller's actions in the same amount of time or less. If the person successfully repeats the Caller's actions, the Caller remains in the circle for another round. If not, the other player becomes the Caller.

Slower players who become Callers can outwit faster players by creating complicated movements. If the group decides that the player copying the Caller didn't copy the original action well enough, he or she becomes the Caller regardless of the time it took to repeat the action. For added difficulty, tell Callers that each action they choose must be something that's not been done before in the game.

# PERSEVERANCE

**NUMBER OF PLAYERS:** Two or more

**LOCATION:** A large field

## THE GAME:
Choose one player and have him or her stand at one end of a large field. Have everyone else stand at a starting line at the other end.

To begin, direct the solo player to turn his or her back to the others and to count to 10 loudly enough for everyone to hear. While the solo player is counting, have everyone else each raise a hand with fingers signaling a number between one and five.

When the solo player finishes counting, he or she is to raise a hand clearly signaling a number between one and five. However, the solo player may not turn around to see the other players. Anyone on the starting line holding up the same number of fingers as the solo player is eliminated from the game and must retire to the sidelines. Everyone else is permitted to take as many steps forward toward the solo player as they held up. The solo player may then turn around to see who has moved closer. Then instruct the solo player to turn around and repeat the process.

For the majority of the players, the object of this game is to survive the eliminations and come close enough to the solo player to reach out and tag him or her. If the solo player retires all the other players without being tagged, he or she wins and remains the solo player. But if the solo player is tagged, the person who tagged him or her gets to be the new solo player for the next round.

Use the following questions to spark discussion after this game. Ask:

● **What did this game teach you about perseverance in the face of bad luck?**

● **In what situations in everyday life must you persevere?**

● **Read Psalm 107:23-31. How can we benefit from trying circumstances in our lives?**

# PREDICTABLE BEHAVIOR

**NUMBER OF PLAYERS:** Six or more

**LOCATION:** Any grassy or sandy area

**THE GAME:** Form two teams. Have members of team 1 huddle together and choose three different physical activities they want team 2 to do. For example, they may ask team 2 to run a lap, jump up and down 10 times, and play leapfrog. Explain that all choices must be physically possible and safe.

While team 1 decides what activities team 2 will do, ask members of team 2 to name the three activities they think team 1 will choose. When both teams have decided, have team 1 tell the group what the activities are. Team 2 wins 1 point for each correct guess, but team members must do the actions they didn't guess. Repeat the activity with teams trading roles. Play for a specified number of rounds or until kids run out of energy. The team with the most points wins.

# ROLLER RELAY

**NUMBER OF PLAYERS:** Eight or more

**LOCATION:** Any grassy or sandy area where kids can roll and tumble without getting hurt

**THE GAME:** Form teams of four or more and have them line up on one side of the playing area. Send half of each team to the other side of the area. On your signal, have one person from each team run to the center of the area, lie down, roll 10 times on the ground, get up, and run to tag a team member on the opposite side of the field. This person should then run to the middle, roll 10 times, and continue the relay by tagging the next person on his or her team. The first team to have all its members complete the relay wins.

# ROPE BUILDER

**NUMBER OF PLAYERS:** Any large group

**LOCATION:** Any playing area in which your group can spread out

**THE GAME:** Form two teams. Then arrange players at random all over the field. Tell players to remain stationary. Instruct members of one team to hold out their left hands and members of the other team to hold out their right hands. Choose a player from each team and send the two players to opposite sides of the field.

On your signal, have the two players you chose run onto the field, extend their hands, and grab the closest players on their teams. Each group must remain connected while it adds the rest of its team members to the "rope" as quickly as possible. The first team to connect all its members wins.

If a rope breaks or grabs a person from the other team, play begins again. But this time, the runner for the offending team must wait one second after your starting signal.

# RUBBER BAND

**NUMBER OF PLAYERS:** Eight or more

**LOCATION:** Any grassy or sandy area

**THE GAME:** Have kids hold hands in a circle. Then tell kids to form shapes (see below) without releasing hands. Keep things moving by calling out new shapes as soon as others are completed. If you have a large group, form teams and have them compete to create the shapes first.

- figure eight
- square
- rectangle
- triangle
- star
- octagon
- diamond
- circle within a circle

# SENSIBLE LANGUAGES

**NUMBER OF PLAYERS:** Five or more

**LOCATION:** Any field or park that's loaded with sights and sounds

**THE GAME:** Form five groups. Tell groups that they represent different tribes with different ways of relating to the world. Assign each group one of the following tribes.

- **The Ear Tribe:** This tribe may describe only the sounds of things. For example, members might describe dogs barking, bees buzzing, or wind whistling in the trees. This tribe may also mimic the sounds of the objects.

- **The Sight Tribe:** This tribe may describe things only in terms of what they look like. Members may not call them by name. For example, they might describe a tree as a tall, brown, wrinkled object.

- **The Touch Tribe:** This tribe may describe things only in terms of what they feel like. Members may not use the actual names of the objects. For example, they might describe a leaf as a soft, flat object with ridges on it.

- **The Motion Tribe:** This tribe may describe things only in terms of how they move. For example, members might describe a duck as a slow, waddling creature. This tribe may also use motions to help describe the object or animal.

- **The Smell Tribe:** This tribe may describe things only by how they smell. For example, members might describe flowers as sweet or dirt as musty.

Have tribes go out to explore the objects and creatures in the field or park. After a specified amount of time, have tribes return and use their tribal "languages" to describe at least 10 things they found. If possible, have each tribe member describe at least one item. While one tribe describes an object, have the others try to guess what it is. Award 1 point to a tribe for each correct guess made by a member of that tribe. If a tribe uses the proper name of the item it's describing, penalize that tribe 1 point. The tribe with the most points wins.

# SWARM TAG

**NUMBER OF PLAYERS:** 12 or more

**LOCATION:** Any large field or open area

**THE GAME:** Form at least three teams of four to 10 players. Tell each team to choose one player to be "It." On your signal, have each team play a game of Tag. Whenever a team member is tagged, he or she becomes It for that team and must call out, "I'm It!"

The catch is that all of the teams must play in the same area. In addition, if someone who's It tags a member of another team, the two players must switch teams and the person who was tagged becomes It for his or her new team. This game will turn into mayhem after a short while, but that's part of the fun. After a set time, stop play and award a round of applause to any team members who were never tagged and are still in their original teams.

# WHIRLWIND

**NUMBER OF PLAYERS:** Six or more

**LOCATION:** Any grassy or sandy area

**THE GAME:** Form teams of three. Choose one team to be "It" and have members of that team hold hands in a circle facing outward. Have other teams hold hands in circles facing inward.

Say: **The object of this Tag game is for the team that's It to tag another team, which then becomes It. The only rule is that a team can't be tagged as long as it's spinning in a circle and team members are holding hands. Teams can move around the playing area, but they must be spinning to avoid being tagged. If a team breaks the circle, stops spinning, or falls down, It can tag them. When a new team becomes It, team members must face outward and try to tag another team. The object is not to be It at the end of the game.**

# WHITEWATER

**NUMBER OF PLAYERS:** 20 or more

**LOCATION:** Any grassy or sandy area

**THE GAME:** Form two teams of equal size. Have one person from each team sit on the ground with legs straight out. Then have another person from the same team sit down next to the first, but facing the opposite direction. Each person's ankles should touch his or her neighbor's hips. Continue in this back and forth fashion until each team has created a long line.

Then have members of each team grab hands with the people next to them to form a continuous wave.

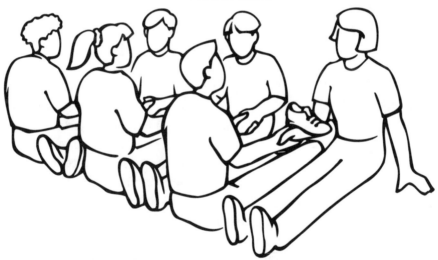

Balance a shoe on one end of each team's wave, then tell the teams to pass the shoes to the other end. Teams may not use their hands to move the shoes. They must pass them along on their arms. Kids will be able to move the shoe by leaning close to each other and moving their arms up and down and left and right. If the shoe falls, the team must place it at the beginning and start again. Have teams race to see which can move the shoe down the "rapids" the fastest.

# WILDFIRE

**NUMBER OF PLAYERS:** 12 or more

**LOCATION:** Any large, open area

**THE GAME:** Choose one person to be Fire and three to be Flames. Form the rest of the group into teams of four. Have members of each team stand in a circle, face outward, and hold hands. Then have all the teams spread out across the playing field at least eight feet from any other team.

Explain that Fire can tag Flames. If Fire tags a Flame, the two players reverse roles. A Flame can escape danger by tagging any person in any circle. When a Flame tags someone, the person directly across from the person tagged must exchange places with the Flame. The object is not to be Fire at the end of the game.

## EAGLE PERCH

**NUMBER OF PLAYERS:** Any number

**LOCATION:** Any fairly empty parking lot

**THE GAME:** When you stop to rest or eat, gather kids around
a concrete parking block or any other object shaped like a balance beam. Then challenge kids with the following competitions.

● See who can balance on the block the longest while standing
on one foot with both arms out like eagle wings and one leg
stretched out in back.

● See who can run along a row of concrete blocks the fastest
without touching the ground.

● See who can hop along a row of concrete blocks without
falling or touching the ground.

● Form teams of no more than four and see which team can
create the most unusual statue with all team members balancing
on the concrete blocks.

## MAD TRAVELERS

**NUMBER OF PLAYERS:** Any number in the same vehicle

**LOCATION:** Any highway

**THE GAME:** This activity gives kids the freedom to be a little
strange for the enjoyment of other travelers on the road and for

# GAMES

*Taking your group on a long trip is often one of the greatest experiences you'll ever have with your teenagers . . . if you can survive the drive. This chapter provides lots of games to help the trip go more smoothly. You'll find everything from riddles and observation games for the road to energy-burning games for rest stops. Use these games to make your travel time just as exciting as your destination.*

their own fun, too. Use the suggestions provided below, then have kids come up with their own ideas. Instruct the group to perform the maneuvers when you pass other vehicles or when other vehicles pass you. For obvious safety reasons, the driver is always exempt from participation.

● Have all the kids turn their heads in unison, first to the left, then straight ahead, then to the right, then straight ahead, and so on.

● Have all the kids on the left side of the vehicle lean their heads forward in unison while all the kids on the right hold theirs up. Then have sides switch positions back and forth.

● Have all the kids move their arms forward and backward in unison as though they're rowing oars on a ship. To enhance the effect, have kids open the windows and sing a song that goes with the beat. This one gets lots of stares at rest stops.

● When you get to a rest stop, have kids leapfrog over each other to the bathrooms. Then have kids leapfrog back to the cars.

● Before you stop, determine what order passengers would need to stand in to go from shortest to tallest. After you stop, have everyone silently line up from shortest to tallest and march to the restrooms, restaurant, or wherever. Repeat the activity on the way back to the vehicle, but this time have the kids walk in a silly way.

# MYSTERIOUS HIGHWAY

**NUMBER OF PLAYERS:** Any number in the same vehicle

**LOCATION:** Any highway

## THE GAME:
In the following games, kids must recognize a "pattern" and thus determine the solution. Explain that kids are to figure out the solution to the game but not tell anyone until everyone has figured it out or a specified time has elapsed. These are just a few of the many variations you can use to occupy kids while on long, boring stretches of the road.

**Guided Tour:** Say: **We're going to combine storytelling with competition and a mystery. One at a time, each of you gets to tell an interesting story about something you see outside the car. For example, the story may involve a landmark such as a barn or a sign. Your story may be completely fictional, completely true, or a little bit of both.**

Explain that kids must talk loudly enough for the leader to hear. The leader will give each person a score immediately after he or she finishes.

Then say: **Before I announce the score for a story, each of you must guess the score you believe I will give that story. The trick is to figure out how the score is determined so you can always guess correctly.**

Here's the secret: Give a score equal to the last digit of the first mile marker you pass after the completion of the story. Don't tell kids the secret until everyone either figures it out or gives up.

**Three Things:** Say: **I'm going to point to three things in plain view, name them, then ask you to guess who is "It." For example, I might point out an old car, Mary's blue button, and a stoplight. Then I'll ask, "Who is It?" Your job is to identify It. After a while, you should be able to identify It for each set of items.**

Here's the secret: The first person to speak after the leader names the objects is It.

If players fail to name It after a few tries, identify It but don't tell them how It was chosen. Play plenty of rounds to see if anyone can figure out the secret to the game.

**Invisible Troll:** Say: **It's well known that many invisible trolls inhabit this highway. If we come to one, you'll hear me call out, "Troll, let us pass!" This is because the trolls are known to cause accidents if you don't ask permission to pass. The object of the game is to figure out how I know when we come to an invisible troll.**

Here's the secret: The leader calls out "Troll, let us pass!" each time a passenger uses the word "out" (or another commonly used word of your choice) in a sentence. For example, a passenger might say, "Have you figured it out?" or "Get outta here!" It's best to wait about five seconds before "identifying" the troll. This game can be tough, so try it after finishing the first two variations. That way kids will know that they're looking for a secret or pattern to solve the puzzle.

# Private Eye

**NUMBER OF PLAYERS:** Any number

**LOCATION:** Any highway

**THE GAME:** Besides being fun, this game gives kids an opportunity to get to know each other better. Secretly instruct each person on your trip to be a private eye responsible to find out some fact about everyone else traveling on the trip. Don't tell kids that anyone else is doing something similar. It's best if each person believes that he or she is the only private eye. Tell the private eyes to get the information without anyone knowing they're looking for it.

Assign one of the following categories to each private eye:

- middle name
- favorite food
- date of birth
- length of time at current address
- town in which he or she attended kindergarten

- birthplace
- favorite school subject
- number of siblings
- favorite television show
- favorite radio station
- longest trip taken

At the end of the trip, have kids form a circle. Then explain that all of the kids were private eyes with different assignments. First, tell kids to guess, based on the questions they were asked, which assignment each person was given. Then have private eyes tell what they discovered. Private eyes whose assignments were not guessed get 2 points for every accurate piece of information they reveal. Private eyes whose assignments were guessed get 1 point for every accurate piece of information.

To make this game work for a large group, form smaller groups of no more than 12 and have kids spy only on members of their groups.

# RAVENS AND CROWS

**NUMBER OF PLAYERS:** Any number in the same vehicle

**LOCATION:** Most rural or semirural areas of North America

**THE GAME:** Ravens and crows are large, black birds that are found year-round in most rural and semirural areas of North America. For this game to work, kids must be able to identify ravens or crows from a distance. Before playing, choose one person to serve as a judge.

Form two teams. Teams will compete to be the first to spot, in order, the items listed on page 75. The judge will determine if kids saw what they claimed to have seen. Any time one team finds an object, the other team can't claim it until it finds another one just like it. The first team to reach the end of the list wins.

However, whenever someone spots a raven or crow, he or she can call out "blackbird" and point to it. If the judge sees the bird and agrees that it's a raven or crow, the other team must go back to the first item on the list and start over. Teams can call "black-bird" only once every two miles. (Keep track of the mileage on the vehicle's odometer.)

---

## ITEM LIST

1. A red car
2. A dead tree (or, in winter, one with broken limbs)
3. A blue trailer
4. A boat
5. Any road kill
6. A wooden fence post
7. A yellow or green bumper sticker
8. A dog (or other animal such as a squirrel, rabbit, or cow)
9. A convertible
10. A billboard with a picture of a human on it
11. A barn (or an abandoned building)
12. A motor home
13. A semitrailer
14. A license plate with the letter J on it
15. An airplane
16. A fast-food sign or billboard
17. A tour bus
18. A train (or train tracks)
19. A license plate from any state at least two states away from the current location
20. A police or highway patrol vehicle with flashing lights

---

# REST-STOP RACES

**NUMBER OF PLAYERS:** Four or more

**LOCATION:** Any highway rest stop

**THE GAME:** Form teams of equal sizes: pairs, small groups, or carloads. Tell teams to race to a specified goal, such as the restroom, and back. Explain that no one can start the race until you signal by honking the horn twice.

Choose a different method for kids to use at each rest stop. For example, at one rest stop you might have kids leapfrog to the goal. At another you might have kids race piggyback or skip.

# RHYME-A-LOG

**NUMBER OF PLAYERS:** Any number in the same vehicle

**LOCATION:** Any highway

**THE GAME:** Instead of having each teenager record trip highlights in a journal, have kids work together to create a poem describing the significant events of the trip. Each time someone comes up with a line, another person must come up with a rhyming line. Then, so kids will memorize the poem by the end of the trip, they must begin at the beginning each time the poem is recited.

To help kids get started, prepare a beginning to the poem yourself. Also, have someone record the poem on paper in case kids forget what they came up with. Here's an example of a few opening lines:

*It was a trip we wouldn't soon forget.*
*We left in rain, and we all got wet.*
*Tim forgot to bring his suitcase.*
*You should have seen the look on his face.*
*Trini gave us all a scare—*
*When we checked the van, she wasn't there!*

Encourage kids to be creative with the poem and to include everyone in the final version. For fun, have kids recite the poem for your congregation.

# RIDDLES

**NUMBER OF PLAYERS:** Any number in the same vehicle

**LOCATION:** Any highway

**THE GAME:** A riddle is nothing more than a word game. Use these to keep kids from getting bored on especially long trips.

To figure out the riddles, kids may ask yes and no questions of the leader. Once a person solves the riddle, he or she should remain silent about the answer until everyone else either solves the riddle or gives up. You'll find the answers to the riddles on page 94.

## RIDDLES

1. A man was going home until he saw a man with a mask. Then the man going home turned and ran away. Why?

2. A woman was lying dead in a field with a soft object on her back. What killed her?

3. Someone claimed to see a man's wife kissing another man just as the full moon rose at midnight in Santa Fe, New Mexico. Why didn't the husband believe this?

4. It is higher than the highest mountain and lower than the lowest valley. What is it?

5. A woman who lived in a skyscraper went home every night, got on the elevator, and rode it up to the 20th floor. Then she got off and climbed the stairs to the 30th floor, where she lived. Every morning, however, she got on the elevator at the 30th floor and rode it all the way down. Why?

6. A man lost in a blizzard found an old cabin with a lantern, a fireplace, and a propane stove. He had only one match. Which did he light first?

7. A woman claimed to have crossed Antarctica with a dog sled, surviving fierce blizzards, extreme cold, and attacks by polar bears. Why didn't anyone believe her?

8. John, Jennifer, and Max were found at the scene of the murder of a man named Peter. The police took John and Jennifer into custody as suspects in the murder but let Max go free. Why?

9. Why didn't a man's relatives bury him west of the Mississippi, even though he lived in California?

10. What can carry water and carry fire?

# ROAD OLYMPICS

**NUMBER OF PLAYERS:** Any number

**LOCATION:** Any rest stop

**THE GAME:** If you're going to be stopping at a number of rest stops on your trip, plan a different athletic contest for each stop. Choose from the following ideas or have kids come up with their own. Have kids who finish first, second, and third stand on a picnic table to receive invisible medals. For added fun, have everyone hum or sing a favorite song or chorus as a tribute to the winner. If you have a large group, form teams and keep track of the accumulated medals for each team so you can declare a champion at the end of the trip.

- See who can collect the most litter in five minutes.
- See who can throw a piece of trash into a receptacle from the greatest distance.
- Race over an obstacle course of picnic tables and trees.
- See who can stand on an empty aluminum soft drink can the longest without crushing it.
- See who can balance the longest on a narrow object or fence.

# STEEPLECHASE

**NUMBER OF PLAYERS:** Any number

**LOCATION:** Any rest stop, campground, or park

**THE GAME:** A steeplechase is a cross-country race with obstacles along the way. To have your group run a steeplechase, quickly designate a course that includes some of the following obstacles: running over or under picnic benches; racing around statues or trees; jogging across foot bridges; leaping over small ditches or holes in the ground; balancing on structures; and climbing over small fences, walls, or other obstacles. Plan a course that doesn't interfere with other travelers, harm wildlife, or endanger your kids. After your group knows the course, collect group members' watches and ask them to predict how long it will take them to complete one or more laps. The winner is the person who comes closest to his or her predicted time.

# $URVEY $AYS...

**NUMBER OF PLAYERS:** Any number in the same vehicle

**LOCATION:** Any highway

**THE GAME:** It's easy for teenagers on a long trip to focus only on the final destination and miss out on the world around them along the way. Use the following idea to help kids enjoy the sights on the way.

Say: **Instead of simply ignoring the world around us as we travel, we're going to make a mental list of significant geographical features along the way. For every 10-mile stretch, you'll need to agree on the most significant feature you've seen.** (You may choose any distance up to 25 miles. For especially long trips, choose a longer distance.) **For particularly boring stretches, it may be nothing more than a tree on the side of the road. For other stretches, it may be a hill or a river or a waterfall. In any case, everyone will need to agree on which feature to include for each stretch.**

If possible, have someone record the choices in a notebook.

At the end of the day, have kids tell which of the stretches they wish they owned and why. For example, someone might choose a stretch that contained a baseball stadium because he or she likes baseball. Another might choose a farmland stretch because he or she likes the outdoors.

# THE PRICE IS RIGHT

**NUMBER OF PLAYERS:** Any number

**LOCATION:** Any convenience or grocery store

**THE GAME:** Have each passenger choose one common grocery item that he or she believes will be available at the store you're heading to. Each person must choose a different item. Then have each person guess what the item will cost in the store.

When you stop at the store, have kids find their items and compare their predictions to the actual prices. The winner is the person who came closest to the actual price.

If you're traveling in several vehicles or have a large group in a van or bus, form teams and total the differences between the predictions and actual prices for each team. The team with the lowest total wins.

# Tour Book

**NUMBER OF PLAYERS:** Any number in the same vehicle

**LOCATION:** Any street or highway

**THE GAME:** Have players race to identify items outside of the vehicle that start with specific letters of the alphabet. Explain that kids are to name things in alphabetical order and may use a name for an object only once. For example, if someone calls out "automobile" and points to a passing car, then calls out "bus" and points to a bus on the highway, other group members may not use "automobile" or "bus" for their A or B words. Allow kids creativity with the letter X. For example, you may want to let them name an item, such as "exit sign," with the letter in it.

As an option, play the same game but have kids look for things which end with specific letters of the alphabet. For example, someone might name a billboard advertising "pizza" for A or a "hub" of a wheel for B.

# Trail Cipher

**NUMBER OF PLAYERS:** Any number traveling or hiking together

**LOCATION:** Any hiking trail

**THE GAME:** Before your group begins a hike along a trail, form pairs. Tell each pair to choose one person to be the "left" partner and the other to be the "right" partner. Then put all the right partners on one team and all left partners on another. Have each team think of a common geographical feature that will be seen along the trail. For example, a team might decide to look for a wildflower, a river or stream, a rock outcropping, or something similar. Have each team choose a feature that will appear occasionally but not every step of the way. Also, have each team choose a secret name by thinking of a verb that may be difficult to slip into normal conversation. For example, a team might choose "disintegrate," "permeate," or "revitalize."

When team members see their geographical features, they must slip into their conversations the secret names for their features. For example, if the secret word is "disintegrate" and the secret item is spotted, someone in the middle of a conversation about school might say, "When I'm outside in a place like this, all my worries about school seem to disintegrate."

The object of the game is for teams to guess each other's secret names and the features they represent.

# TRAVELER TALES

**NUMBER OF PLAYERS:** Any number in the same vehicle

**LOCATION:** Any street or highway with lots of signs and billboards

**THE GAME:** The following games involve creative storytelling. Have your group choose the most original, the most humorous, and the most creative stories for each game.

**Seven Words:** Have passengers take turns telling short stories as you travel down the road. Before each storyteller begins, have the rest of the group choose seven words found on signs outside the vehicle. The storyteller then must use those words in his or her story.

**Fractured Fairy Tale:** Have kids work together to create a fairy tale, with each person adding one sentence at a time. However, every sentence must include at least one noun or verb from a sign or billboard seen outside the vehicle.

**Colorful Tale:** Have kids take turns adding to a story in which every sentence includes a color. For example, someone might begin with "It was a black and stormy night."

**The Rest of the Story:** Have teenagers take turns making up stories about the people in passing cars. Instruct kids to tell who the people are, where they're from, where they're heading, and what they do for a living. Remind kids to be creative, but kind.

# TRAVELERS AWARDS

**NUMBER OF PLAYERS:** Any number

**LOCATION:** Any trip or retreat

**THE GAME:** Before you leave, announce that awards will be given in a number of categories at the end of the trip. Use the categories listed below or create your own. At the end of your trip, have kids vote for one or more winners for each category.

- Friendliest traveler(s)
- Best humorist(s)
- Best entertainer(s)
- Best dishwasher(s)
- Best cheerleader(s)
- Best environmentalist(s)
- Best servant(s)

# WORLD-TOUR ALPHABET

**NUMBER OF PLAYERS:** Any number in the same vehicle

**LOCATION:** Any street or highway

**THE GAME:** Have someone begin the game by naming a geographical place, such as a city, country, river, continent, or ocean, that starts with the letter A. Instruct the next person to name another place that also starts with A. Continue until everyone has named a different place that starts with A. Repeat the process with the next letter until the group completes the entire alphabet.

Anyone who can't think of a place name for the letter may pass. If three people pass on a letter, tell the group to begin again with the next letter in the alphabet. You may want to allow kids to take some liberties with the letter X.

You can also play this game by asking kids to name things such as movies, books, songs, plants, celebrities, animals, or first names.

# CIRCLE, LINE, DOTS

**NUMBER OF PLAYERS:** Nine or more

**LOCATION:** Any room that can be completely darkened

**THE GAME:** Form three to six teams of at least three members each. When you turn off the lights, have each team form a circle (team members hold hands in a circle), a line (team members hold hands in a straight line), or a series of dots (team members stand near each other but don't touch each other). Then turn on the lights.

Award a point to any team that chose a shape no other team chose. For example, if three teams chose circles, two chose lines, and one chose dots, the team that chose dots wins 1 point. If two teams chose unique shapes, each gets a point. No points are awarded if a shape is selected by two or more teams.

Play for a specified length of time or until one team gets 10 points.

# CIRCLES

**NUMBER OF PLAYERS:** Fourteen or more

**LOCATION:** Any large room with easily accessible light switches that turn on and off quickly

**THE GAME:** Choose two people to act as referees. Then form two or more teams of at least six players each. Teach teams how to form

**84**

# AMES

*Ever been with a group of teenagers when the lights suddenly went out? There's something about darkness that sends kids off into another world. Some love it, others fear it. But most enjoy the challenge of games that take away the advantage of sight. Here are a few games to add fun and relationship-building to your night meetings (and dark rooms).*

each of the shapes described in the "Shapes" box below and on page 86.

To start a round, have team members stand sideways in a circle. Instruct one referee to stand by the light switch with his or her back to the teams. Tell this referee to turn off the lights and count out loud to 10. While the lights are off, each team must silently move to create one of the shapes. If anyone other than the referee says a word, the lights go on and the round is canceled.

After counting to 10, the referee can turn on the lights immediately or after waiting several seconds. As soon as the lights come on, everyone must freeze. Then have the other referee award points to the teams according to the shapes they've formed. No points should be awarded to any team that fails to form a shape completely or moves after the lights go on.

Continue play for a number of rounds, but tell teams that they may not create the same shape twice in a row. The team with the highest score after a specified number of rounds or length of time wins.

## SHAPES

- **Inside Circle:** Team members face the center of the circle and hold hands. Award 1 point.

- **Outside Circle:** Team members face away from the center of the circle and hold hands. Award 1 point.

- **Starburst:** Team members stand in a circle in which they alternate facing inward or outward. To form the shape of a pointed starburst, everyone must lean backward: Those facing inward must lean out, and those facing outward must lean in. If a team has an uneven number of members, one team member must stand in the middle of the circle while the others form this shape. Award 5 points.

- **Woven Circle:** Team members face the center of the circle with their hands at their sides. Then, team members raise their right hands and hold them in front of their neighbors. Next, they raise their left hands, reach under the right arms in front of them, and grasp the hands in front of their neighbors to the left. If done correctly, they'll form a woven circle with all left arms underneath all right arms. Award 15 points.

This game often sparks good discussions about communication. Use the following questions to get participants talking. Ask:

- **How did you react to this game?**
- **When have you reacted that way in everyday life?**
- **What ways did you communicate in this game?**
- **How can you use similar ideas in everyday life?**
- **Read Mark 8:22-25. How are you learning to see and know God more clearly?**

# CODE BLUE, CODE RED

**NUMBER OF PLAYERS:** Six or more

**LOCATION:** Any area, inside or outside, where kids can mill about in darkness without risk of injury

**THE GAME:** Form two teams and designate one the Red team and the other the Blue team. In a darkened room or outside area where visibility is limited but the playing surface is safe, have everyone mill around and try to tag each other. Tell kids that no talking is allowed.

Explain that Red team members must tag on the right shoulder and Blue team members must tag on the left shoulder. Whenever a person is tagged, he or she becomes a member of the tagging team and must and start tagging others on the appropriate shoulder. In the dark, kids may inadvertently tag the wrong shoulder, but that's OK. It just adds to the fun!

After about five minutes, gather everyone together in the light and see which team has the most members.

# CRICKETS

**NUMBER OF PLAYERS:** Six to 24

**LOCATION:** Any large, dark area

**THE GAME:** Make sure kids know each other's names. Then form two teams. Assign each team one side of the playing area and choose one team to go first. Tell teams to secretly decide the order in which team members will take their turns.

To start play, tell members of the first team to spread themselves out on their side of the playing area. Then have the first player on that team make any kind of clicking sound with his or her tongue.

Instruct members of the second team to agree upon who made the sound. If they guess correctly, direct the second person on the first team to make a clicking sound and the second team to guess who that person is. Continue until the second team makes a wrong guess. When the second team guesses incorrectly, tell teams to switch roles so that the first team huddles up again and the second team spreads out on its side of the playing area.

Continue play back and forth until one team correctly guesses the order of players on the other team. Team members may choose different locations each round, but they must always "click" in the same order.

# HIDDEN TREASURE

**NUMBER OF PLAYERS:** Six or more

**LOCATION:** A dark outdoor area with obstacles such as shrubs and trees that people can hide behind

**THE GAME:** Form two teams and have each team pick one member to be its Treasure. Assign one end of the playing area to each team. Begin the game by having the teams hide their Treasures somewhere in their playing areas.

After both Treasures are hidden, instruct team members to cross over into each other's playing areas to search for the opposing team's Treasure. The first team to find the other Treasure and call out "I've found the Treasure!" wins.

To add variety, have each team choose a different person as the Treasure for each round or allow the Treasures to move around while the teams are looking for them. Declare the winning team the one whose Treasure avoids detection the longest out of all of the rounds.

# NIGHT AND DAY

**NUMBER OF PLAYERS:** Two or more

**LOCATION:** Any outdoor area your group hasn't seen before

**THE GAME:** Form small groups and send them out at night into an unfamiliar, but safe, natural area. If possible, send each small group out into a different area.

Allow enough time for group members to explore the area with all five of their senses. After everyone returns, have members of each small group describe the area to the whole group. Ask kids how their descriptions might have been different if they had been exploring during the daylight.

For added insight, have kids revisit the same locations the following day. As before, send them out in groups to explore. Have groups report all the things they missed while exploring the previous night.

Use the following questions to spark discussion after this activity. Ask:

- **What did this experience teach you about your perceptions?**
- **How is the daytime a different world from the nighttime?**
- **Read Psalm 139:7-12. How do we perceive night and day differently from the way God perceives them?**

# NIGHT HUNTER

**NUMBER OF PLAYERS:** Six or more

**LOCATION:** Any outdoor location where players can move about safely in semidarkness

**THE GAME:** Privately assign each teenager to one of the following teams: Wolf, Snake, Human. As much as possible, make the teams the same size.

Then have team members spread out around the area. On your signal, have kids move around and try to capture each other using the following rules of capture.

● When someone is tagged, both parties must make their species' sounds: Wolves howl, Snakes hiss, and Humans say "human."

● Capture is determined by the following rules: Snake captures human, human captures Wolf, and Wolf captures snake.

● Once a player is captured, he or she must go to a neutral area and sit down until the game ends.

Play for five minutes or so. The object is to capture the most players without being caught. Attentive players will observe other interactions to determine the identity of the other animals.

**Bear Option:** In this option, choose one person to be the Bear. The Bear is to identify himself or herself with a growl. The Bear can capture others but cannot be captured by others. The object for everyone else is to capture as many others as possible without being captured by the Bear.

# NIGHT OWL

**NUMBER OF PLAYERS:** 12 or more

**LOCATION:** Any location where people can move about safely in the dark with lots of places to hide

**THE GAME:** Form teams of six to eight, then appoint one person in each team to be the Owl. Have the Owl and the rest of his or her team agree on a call that the rest of the team can use to find the Owl in the darkness. Advise teams to make their Owl calls unique so they won't be confused with other teams' calls.

Then send all the Owls to hide. Once Owls are hidden, send teams out making the Owl calls. Any Owl who hears his or her team's call must reply with the same call.

Owls can move about in the darkness as often as they wish, changing hiding places until they're found. The goal for the Owls is to be the last Owl found by his or her team. The goal for each team is to be the first to find its Owl. Kids may imitate other teams' calls to throw them off the track.

# SECRET CROSSING

**NUMBER OF PLAYERS:** Six or more

**LOCATION:** Any large room with easy access to lights that switch on and off quickly

**THE GAME:** Form two teams: team 1 and team 2. Place team 1 near the light switch. Designate a starting place and an ending place somewhere in the room.

While team 1 works the light switch, have team 2 try to silently sneak its players from the starting place to the ending place. When a member of team 1 is suspicious that someone from team 2 is moving, he or she may turn on the lights. For each person caught moving between the starting and ending place, team 1 earns 1 point. If no one is between the starting and ending points when the light is switched on, team 2 gets 1 point. In addition, team 2 gets 1 point for each team member who successfully gets to the ending place without being caught.

Have teams switch roles and play an equal number of rounds of up to four minutes each. The team with the most points at the end wins the game.

# STRANGER IN THE NIGHT

**NUMBER OF PLAYERS:** Six or more

**LOCATION:** Any completely dark room

**THE GAME:** Have kids mill around in the dark. Walk around among the kids and tap one person on the shoulder and another on the hand. Wait several moments, then have everyone sit down.

After everyone is seated, direct the person you tapped on the shoulder to say one word in a disguised voice. Then have the person you tapped on the hand guess who spoke the word. If the guess is incorrect, the guesser must leave the game. If the guess is correct, the person who spoke the word must leave the game. Continue play in this manner until only two people remain. They're the winners.

# SWITCH

**NUMBER OF PLAYERS:** Four or more

**LOCATION:** Any large room with easy access to light switches

**THE GAME:** Form two teams and have them line up facing each other. With the lights on, have team members closely examine every member of the opposing team. Then turn off the lights and tell each team to huddle. During the huddle, have two members of each team exchange one item of clothing or jewelry that was completely visible to their opponents (as long as the item doesn't compromise decency). Players can trade the same object, such as a belt for a belt or shoes for shoes, or different objects such as a watch for a belt.

When teams are ready, have them re-form their lines. Then turn on the lights and allow each team one guess as to which two items were traded on the other team. Award 1 point for each correct guess. The team with the most points after a set number of rounds is the winner.

# WAKING DREAM

**NUMBER OF PLAYERS:** Three to 36

**LOCATION:** Any darkened room or outside area at night

**THE GAME:** Form a circle and explain that you're going to create a dream. Have the first person in the circle give a one-sentence description of a scene appropriate to a dream. Then have the person to his or her right add another sentence describing the dream. Continue around the circle until each person has added to the dream. As in real dreams, the logical link between scenes doesn't need to be strong. Go around the circle more than once if you have a small group. You may want to give kids a dream category—such as adventure, humor, sports, vacation, or food—and have them build dreams using this category.

End the game by having each student share one real dream that he or she has had.

# ANSWERS

## "MURDER MYSTERY"

**(CHAPTER 3, PAGE 49):** Suspect Three killed Lady Chantel Hawkins with a harpoon at the Great Wall of China.

## "RIDDLES"

**(CHAPTER 5, PAGE 76):**

1. He turned and ran because the man with the mask was a baseball catcher, and someone had thrown the ball to the catcher while the man was trying to steal home.

2. Her parachute failed to open.

3. The full moon never rises at midnight in Santa Fe, New Mexico, or anywhere else, for that matter.

4. Water. Water vapor rises in the atmosphere above all mountains and lies in wells beneath the deepest valleys.

5. The woman was too short to reach any elevator button higher than the one for the 20th floor.

6. He lit the match first.

7. There are no polar bears in Antarctica.

8. Max was a dog.

9. He wasn't dead yet.

10. Pipes. Pipes used in plumbing carry water, and pipes used for smoking carry fire.

# Evaluation of
# No Supplies Required Crowdbreakers & Games

Please help Group Publishing, Inc. continue providing innovative and usable resources for ministry by taking a moment to fill out and send us this evaluation. Thanks!

● ● ●

1. As a whole, this book has been (circle one)

Not much help                                    Very helpful

1     2     3     4     5     6     7     8     9     10

2. The things I liked best about this book were:

3. This book could be improved by:

4. One thing I'll do differently because of this book is:

5. Optional Information:

Name _____

Street Address _____

City _____ State _____ Zip _____

Phone Number _____ Date _____

Bible Study Series

# Give Your Teenagers a Solid Faith Foundation That Lasts a Lifetime!

Here are the *essentials* of the Christian life—core values teenagers *must* believe to make good decisions now...and build an *unshakable* lifelong faith. Developed by youth workers like you...field-tested with *real* youth groups in *real* churches...here's the meat your kids *must* have to grow spiritually—presented in a fun, involving way!

Each 4-session **Core Belief Bible Study Series** book lets you easily...

- •Lead deep, compelling, *relevant* discussions your kids won't want to miss...
- •Involve teenagers in exploring life-changing truths...
- •Ground your teenagers in God's Word...and
- •Help kids create healthy relationships with each other—and you!
- •**Plus you'll make an *eternal difference* in the lives of your kids** as you give them a solid faith foundation that stands firm on God's Word.

## Here are the Core Belief Bible Study Series titles already available...

### Senior High Studies

| | |
|---|---|
| Why **Being a Christian** Matters | 0-7644-0883-6 |
| Why **Creation** Matters | 0-7644-0880-1 |
| Why **God** Matters | 0-7644-0874-7 |
| Why **Jesus Christ** Matters | 0-7644-0875-5 |
| Why **Spiritual Growth** Matters | 0-7644-0884-4 |
| Why **Suffering** Matters | 0-7644-0879-8 |
| Why the **Bible** Matters | 0-7644-0882-8 |
| Why the **Holy Spirit** Matters | 0-7644-0876-3 |
| Why the **Spiritual Realm** Matters | 0-7644-0881-X |

### Junior High/Middle School Studies

| | |
|---|---|
| The Truth About **Being a Christian** | 0-7644-0859-3 |
| The Truth About **Creation** | 0-7644-0856-9 |
| The Truth About **God** | 0-7644-0850-X |
| The Truth About **Jesus Christ** | 0-7644-0851-8 |
| The Truth About **Spiritual Growth** | 0-7644-0860-7 |
| The Truth About **Suffering** | 0-7644-0855-0 |
| The Truth About the **Bible** | 0-7644-0858-5 |
| The Truth About the **Holy Spirit** | 0-7644-0852-6 |
| The Truth About the **Spiritual Realm** | 0-7644-0857-7 |